STEPHEN
KING

STEPHEN KING

His Life, Work, and Influences

BEV VINCENT

becker&mayer! kids

CONTENTS

FOREWORD
THANKS FOR THE RIDE, STEPHEN!

My first introduction to Stephen King wasn't from a book or short story but rather an accidental viewing of *Creepshow 2—The Hitchhiker*.

I was around nine years old when we stopped in to say hi to my aunt and uncle in Saint John, New Brunswick in Canada. They were watching *Creepshow 2* and forgot to turn the television off. My younger sister and I snuck into the living room and were greeted by Annie repeatedly running over that hitchhiker who would thank her for the ride every time. The phrase "Thanks for the ride, lady" became a core memory that haunted my dreams growing up and is a long-standing family joke.

Once I was a little older my mom would offer me King titles to read, but I would turn them down in fear that the combination of his writing and my imagination would become too much. Years later when I became an English teacher, I decided that my main goal was for students to leave my classroom having the belief that they too could love to read. I am always looking for ideas on how to better entice students to love reading as much as I do; it is a matter of finding the right author, theme, or subject to appeal to the reader to get them interested. And King's writing ticks every box!

The original idea to try to convince Stephen King to visit Sussex Regional High School in Sussex, New Brunswick, Canada came to fellow teachers Phyllis Corbett, Bonny Hill, Patricia Stout, and Stacey Eisner on a visit to Maine over the summer of 2011. I am forever indebted to them for letting me take their crazy idea and run with it. I was intrigued and thought that it would be amazing if we as educators could achieve something with our students that many viewed as impossible.

For an entire year, we embarked on a school-wide literacy campaign centered around Stephen King's work. Students not only read King, but created their own short films, parody music videos, and various artwork inspired by his stories. They also put effort into writing over 1,200 persuasive letters aimed at convincing King to visit our school to be sent to King along with their creative work.

We were met with success in October of 2012 when Stephen King came to visit the school. King worked with around twenty students in a closed writing workshop in our school library where he read their work and gave valuable suggestions and direction; King also took home writing pieces from some of the students and mailed them back to them with handwritten feedback. After the hour-long workshop, King met with around eighty students where he read a section from the book *Christine*, talked about growing up in Maine, becoming a writer, and answered students' questions about his writing process, where he got his inspirations from, and if he ever thinks he wrote something that was "too much." King stayed at the school for around three hours (under the radar of the media) and the culinary students made him a brown bag lunch for his drive back to Maine. When asked what drove him to make the trip, King answered, "I came because of all those letters. I was just blissed out to get them all."

I am thrilled to welcome you into the world of Stephen King! His works are great for young readers due to the complex themes they explore. Even though the stories are fiction, the themes reflect real-life struggles and inner conflicts that you might connect with, finding reflections of your own challenges within these narratives. As a young reader, some themes in King's works you might explore could be coming-of-age struggles; social isolation and belonging; mental health; revenge; friendship; faith; and choice. These are issues young people confront daily, allowing you to engage with these stories on a deeper level, providing a safe space to reflect and connect. In discussing these themes in the classroom, with fellow King readers and friends, or in a reading group, you can engage, question, and relate to the narrative. See your own fears, hopes, and dreams reflected in the characters and situations King creates, and tackle these issues in a meaningful and insightful way to enhance your understanding of the literature and create a deeper understanding of yourself and the world around you.

If you're looking for recommendations on where to start with King, some of my favorites are *11/22/63*, *The Girl Who Loved Tom Gordon*, *The Green Mile*, and *The Gunslinger*. Also consider King's short stories "Here There Be Tygers," "Graveyard Shift," "The Last Rung on the Ladder," "Suffer the Little Children," and "Word Processor of the Gods."

Happy reading and, when you see Annie, make sure to thank her for the ride.

SARAH-JANE SMITH

Sarah-Jane Smith has been teaching high school for over fifteen years. She holds a Master of Education in Curriculum and Instruction, and can often be found in her classroom at Kennebecasis Valley High School in New Brunswick, Canada discussing books and stories with her students.

INTRODUCTION

Mobs of fans flock to Bangor, Maine every October. They're hoping that Stephen King has opened his supposedly haunted house to the public for Halloween. However, the author, who stated he had become the "Santa Claus of Halloween," ended this tradition long ago after it became too overwhelming.

Even when it isn't Halloween, fans gather on the street outside his home, peering through the wrought-iron gates decorated with metalwork bats and spiders, in hopes of catching a glimpse of the famous author.

Stephen King's name means horror, and his creations have become icons of the genre. Bad prom dates are described with references to *Carrie*. Scary dogs are called Cujo. Mishaps involving self-driving cars invariably mention *Christine*.

While other contemporary writers may sell as many or more copies of new books as Stephen King does (J. K. Rowling and R. L. Stine come to mind), no one else symbolizes an entire genre the way Stephen King does. He almost single-handedly created a booming market for horror fiction where there was none before. In part, it was a matter of being in the right place at the right time. Readers who had experienced the terrors of *The Exorcist* were ready for more, and Stephen King delivered. By the time his third novel, *The Shining*, hit the bestseller lists, Stephen King was already being called "the master of modern horror." Almost overnight, he had become a "brand name" author.

Stephen King's Bangor home, the William Arnold House, styled after an Italianate villa, stands behind a wrought-iron fence decorated with bats, spiders, and webs.

However, very few of the other authors writing at that time are still household names,[1] which proves that his success wasn't due only to good timing. The brilliance of Stephen King's storytelling has landed him at the top of bestseller lists time and time again. Regardless of the state of the horror genre over the years, Stephen King has continued to thrive. Also, he doesn't limit his writing to the genre for which he is best known. In recent years, he has published award-winning crime novels, and his greatest achievement is a long fantasy series. He is in a class all by himself.

Stephen King has been on a unique journey, from poor university student to struggling schoolteacher to one of the bestselling—and most recognizable—authors of all time. He has embraced every innovation technology has offered, both in publishing and in promoting his work. In the 1990s, he experimented with electronic publishing long before it was popular. In the twenty-first century, he is using Zoom interviews, X (Twitter), YouTube promo clips, and animated comics to find new audiences for his work and reach his scores of fans.

In addition to being the author of novels, short stories, and essays, he is a screenwriter, film producer, movie director, and actor. He has appeared in TV commercials, been featured on the cover of *Time* magazine, founded charities, won prestigious awards, and has—at last—received critical acclaim for his work.

Hardly a year has gone by since the mid-1970s without one of Stephen King's books appearing on a bestseller list or with an adaptation playing in theaters or on a streaming service. However, it isn't just great marketing that keeps readers screaming for more. His long-term success is a testament to the irresistible grip his writing has on millions of readers.

While readers may feel they know Stephen King, it is important to remember that novelists make things up for a living. Even—perhaps especially—when they are writing about their own experiences, they can't resist the temptation to improve on the story. This book captures many of the events that inspired Stephen King's works, using his novels as a lens through which to observe his life. The personal memorabilia included provides a special look into the life and creations of the "master of horror."

CHAPTER 1

The Future Artist As A Young Man (1950-1969)

It's said that Stephen King burst onto the publishing scene when *Carrie* was published in 1974. While there is a bit of truth to that, the often-told tale ignores the hard work Stephen had been doing before *Carrie* came along. By the time that book appeared, he had been writing for almost twenty years and had been a published author for a decade.

Stephen King was born in Portland, Maine, on September 21, 1947. His parents, Donald and Ruth King, had an adopted son, David, who was two at the time. When Stephen was just two years old, his father abandoned the family and was never heard from again. Stephen's mother took unskilled and low-paid jobs to support her family. The family moved around a lot, living in Wisconsin, Indiana, and Connecticut. Stephen missed most of his first year of school because of a severe case of tonsillitis. It caused infections that required painful ear-lancing procedures. Stephen spent most of that year in bed. Since the family didn't own a television, he had to rely on his imagination to entertain himself.

"My childhood was pretty ordinary, except from a very early age I wanted to be scared. My imagination was very active even at a young age," he said. "For instance, there was a radio program at the time called *Dimension X*, and my mother didn't want me to listen to that because she felt it was too scary for me, so I would creep out of bed and go to the bedroom door and crack it open. And she loved it, so apparently, I got it from her, but I would listen at the door and then when the program was over I'd go back to bed and quake."[2]

LEFT: Ruth King with her two sons, David and Stephen, in Portland, Maine, early 1948. BELOW: King and his brother, Dave, circa 1953, in their front yard in Fort Wayne, Indiana, where their father's family lived.

Stephen became a bookworm and started to write stories at the age of six. His earliest attempts at writing fiction involved creating prose versions of the comics he was reading, adding his own descriptions to text he copied. When his mother discovered what Stephen was doing, she told him he should be making up his own stories instead. So he wrote about "four magic animals who rode around in an old car, helping out little kids. Their leader was a large white bunny named Mr. Rabbit Trick. He got to drive the car."[3] His mother told him the story was good enough to be in a book. Stephen's Aunt Gert was amused by his story-writing hobby and paid him a quarter a story.

The family eventually settled in Durham, Maine. There Stephen started a series of projects that foretold his future as a creative and innovative writer. In 1960, he and his new friend Chris Chesley published a collection of one-page stories entitled *People, Places, and Things*. Only one of these tales, "The Hotel at the End of the Road," has ever been reprinted, and only a single copy of the original collection reportedly exists, owned by Stephen himself.

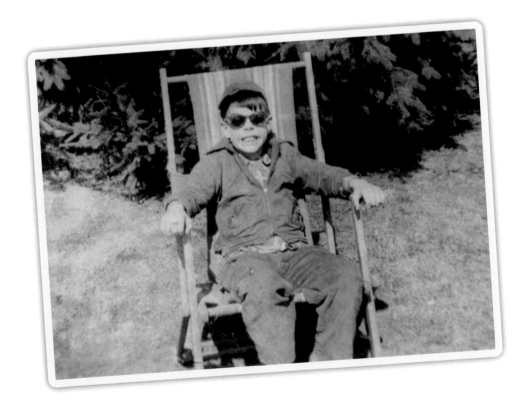

OPPOSITE: King in a lawn chair, mid-1950s. ABOVE: An undated photo from the 1960s showing the young man with his dog.

In the winter of 1959–60, Stephen wrote serialized stories for his brother's neighborhood newspaper, *Dave's Rag*. The following year, Stephen used David's printing press in the basement to produce a twelve-page "novelization" of "The Pit and the Pendulum." The work was based on a Roger Corman movie (based on a story by Edgar Allan Poe) Stephen and Chris had just seen. Stephen figured if he could sell ten copies to his friends at school, the profit after paying for printing supplies and paper would pay for his next trip to the movies. If he sold a dozen copies, he could get popcorn and a soda, too. Stephen's idea was a success, and he later noted, "When I took them to school, I was just flabbergasted. In three days, I sold something like seventy of these things. . . . That was my first experience with bestsellerdom."[4]

However, this early venture in self-publishing came to the attention of the school faculty, and Stephen was forced to return the money he had collected from his classmates. "They took me to the principal's office and told me to stop, although there didn't seem to be any real reason. My aunt taught in that school, and it just was not seemly; it wasn't right. So I had to quit."[5] Stephen was pleased to discover, however, that many of his customers asked to keep their contraband copies of the book.

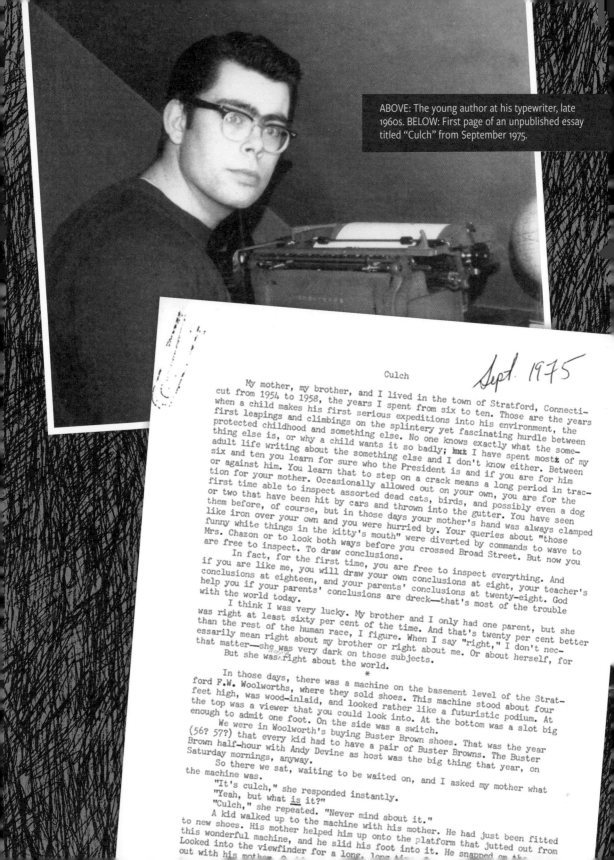

Culch

Sept. 1975

My mother, my brother, and I lived in the town of Stratford, Connecticut from 1954 to 1958, the years I spent from six to ten. Those are the years when a child makes his first serious expeditions into his environment, the first leapings and climbings on the splintery yet fascinating hurdle between protected childhood and something else. No one knows exactly what the something else is, or why a child wants it so badly; but I have spent most of my adult life writing about the something else and I don't know either. Between six and ten you learn for sure who the President is and if you are for him or against him. You learn that to step on a crack means a long period in traction for your mother. Occasionally allowed out on your own, you are for the first time able to inspect assorted dead cats, birds, and possibly even a dog or two that have been hit by cars and thrown into the gutter. You have seen them before, of course, but in those days your mother's hand was always clamped like iron over your own and you were hurried by. Your queries about "those funny white things in the kitty's mouth" were diverted by commands to wave to Mrs. Chazon or to look both ways before you crossed Broad Street. But now you are free to inspect. To draw conclusions.

In fact, for the first time, you are free to inspect everything. And if you are like me, you will draw your own conclusions at eight, your teacher's conclusions at eighteen, and your parents' conclusions at twenty-eight. God help you if your parents' conclusions are dreck—that's most of the trouble with the world today.

I think I was very lucky. My brother and I only had one parent, but she was right at least sixty per cent of the time. And that's twenty per cent better than the rest of the human race, I figure. When I say "right," I don't necessarily mean right about my brother or right about me. Or about herself, for that matter—she was very dark on those subjects.

But she was right about the world.

*

In those days, there was a machine on the basement level of the Stratford F.W. Woolworths, where they sold shoes. This machine stood about four feet high, was wood-inlaid, and looked rather like a futuristic podium. At the top was a viewer that you could look into. On the side was a switch. At the bottom was a slot big enough to admit one foot.

We were in Woolworth's buying Buster Brown shoes. That was the year (56? 57?) that every kid had to have a pair of Buster Browns. The Buster Brown half-hour with Andy Devine as host was the big thing that year, on Saturday mornings, anyway.

So there we sat, waiting to be waited on, and I asked my mother what the machine was.

"It's culch," she responded instantly.

"Yeah, but what _is_ it?"

"Culch," she repeated. "Never mind about it."

A kid walked up to the machine with his mother. He had just been fitted to new shoes. His mother helped him up onto the platform that jutted out from this wonderful machine, and he slid his foot into it. He snapped on the Looked into the viewfinder for a long, long time.

When he was twelve, Stephen found a box of science-fiction and horror paperback novels from the 1940s in his Aunt Ethelyn's attic. The books had been left behind by his father, who had also tried his hand at writing horror stories. This wasn't Stephen's first encounter with horror, but it was his first encounter with serious fantasy horror fiction. A week later, the books disappeared, probably courtesy of his aunt. Although the books were gone, their impact remained.

By the time he was thirteen, Stephen was confident enough to submit his writing for publication. He sent a one-page story called "The Killer" to *Spacemen* magazine, which billed itself as "the world's only space-movie magazine." It wasn't published then, but the publisher kept the manuscript. Decades later, he asked Stephen to sign the page. Stephen recognized the manuscript immediately—he had handwritten in the letter *N* throughout, due to his defective typewriter.

In 1963, Stephen completed his longest piece of writing to date, a 50,000-word novel called *The Aftermath*. Set in a postapocalyptic world where a militaristic organization is trying to establish a new world order with the assistance of a sophisticated supercomputer, it bears some of the hallmarks of his later work. *The Aftermath* is the work of a teenager that will almost certainly never see the light of day, but it does demonstrate Stephen's determination and ability at a young age to complete a novel.

In June 1964, Stephen published a 4,000-word story called "The Star Invaders." The story is dedicated "To Johnny, who wanted one like this," indicating Stephen was willing to write stories specifically to entertain his friends—just like Gordie LaChance does in Stephen's novella *The Body*.

Two more short stories, "Codename: Mousetrap" and "The 43rd Dream," were published in 1965 and 1966, respectively, in the Lisbon High School newspaper, *The Drum*. Stephen edited the paper, although he said: "*The Drum* did not prosper under my editorship. Then as now, I tend to go through periods of idleness followed by periods of workaholic frenzy."[6] Issues of the newspaper containing these stories have turned up in recent years, but the stories have never appeared anywhere else.

Stephen once again found himself in trouble with school authorities when he turned his talents to a parody of *The Drum* called *The Village Vomit*. It featured made-up stories about the school's faculty. This time he received detention—after apologizing to the faculty members featured in the stories. Recognizing his talent for and his love of writing, some of his teachers tried to find ways to channel his creative energy. His guidance counselor urged him to take a job writing sports for the *Lisbon Enterprise*, the Lisbon Falls local newspaper.

Stephen received countless rejection letters from magazines such as *Alfred Hitchcock's Mystery Magazine*. (He hung the rejection slips from a spike on his bedroom wall.) Finally, "I Was a Teenage Grave Robber" was published in installments in the fanzine *Comics Review* in 1965. The following year it was reprinted in another fanzine, *Stories of Suspense*, with a new title, "In a Half-World of Terror."

In 1966, while a high school senior, Stephen wrote the first forty pages of a novel called *Getting It On*, about a student who kills his teacher and takes his classmates hostage. "I suppose if it had been written today, and some high school English teacher had seen it, he would have rushed the manuscript to the guidance counselor and I would have found myself in therapy," he later said. "But 1965 was a different world, one where you didn't have to take off your shoes before boarding a plane and there were no metal detectors at the entrances to high schools."[7]

With his poor eyesight, it was unlikely Stephen would have passed the military physical that would have gotten him drafted to serve in the Vietnam War, but Ruth King wasn't taking any chances. She insisted her son go to college, so in 1966 he started attending the University of Maine. Stephen received scholarships and loans and continued to write while working odd jobs on and off campus.

He wrote an opinion piece for the university newspaper, the *Maine Campus*, in November 1967. In it he expressed his support for the war in Vietnam, with reservations. That same year, at the age of twenty, Stephen made his first professional sale for a piece of his writing, selling "The Glass Floor" to *Startling Mystery Stories* for $30.

However, more than anything, Stephen longed to write and publish novels. Inspired by a series of fifty-mile hikes sponsored by radio and TV stations, he'd written *The Long Walk* in the fall of 1966 and the spring of 1967 when he was a college freshman. Stephen didn't have a car at the time and the idea for the story occurred to him while he was hitchhiking back home one night. "I was hitchhiking everywhere," he says on his website. "I didn't finish my fifty-mile hike, though. I fell out after twenty miles."[8]

Encouraged by the response he received from members of the English Department, Stephen entered it in a first-novel competition run by the publisher Random House. However, the submission was rejected without comment, which discouraged him from sending the manuscript to other publishers.

THE POETRY OF STEPHEN KING

Stephen has a deep and varied interest in poetry. He often quotes poems during interviews, and his work contains references to poets such as Keats and Shelley.

As an undergraduate at the University of Maine in the late 1960s, Stephen wrote forty or fifty poems for a special seminar called Contemporary Poetry. Few of these poems still exist, but Stephen published several of them in the university's literary magazines. The first, "Harrison State Park '68," consisting of approximately one hundred lines of free verse with random indents across the pages, appeared in the Fall 1968 edition of *Ubris*.

Six of his early poems were collected in *The Devil's Wine*, an out-of-print anthology of horror writers' poetry. Reviewing the book, *Publishers Weekly* singled out King's contributions, saying his poems were "good enough to make readers hope the Master Spellbinder revisits his muse more frequently."[9]

Over the years, King has included poems in some of his short story collections or published them in literary magazines. Several others appear in his novels as the work of his characters. In the introduction to the poem "The Bone Church," Stephen says, "I'm not much of a poet. . . . When I do manage something I like, it's mostly by accident."[10]

Many of King's characters write poetry, including Carrie White, Jim Gardener from *The Tommyknockers*, and Holly Gibney from *Mr. Mercedes*. One of the best-known poems in his novels is the haiku attributed to eleven-year-old Ben Hanscom in *It*.

Your hair is winter fire
January embers
My heart burns there, too.

From King's archives, page one of a poem called "Imaginary Places." Some sources suggest it was not written by King.

Imaginary Places

Here are places where United doesn't fly any friendly skies,
  where the railways run down silver tracks of moonlight.
Here are places, you know where no one has ever seen a Spaulding
      tennis racket cover
or a shirt with an alligator on the tit.
"You can't get there from here," the old Maine joke goes,
  and although you can get to Brewer from anywhere--
if you should want to go--
you can only reach these places as if through a wardrobe
and no travel agent sends you to a place through a closet.
    But it's wonderful, you know,
that moment when the unseen wooden floor goes cold and white beneath your
    feet
and the wool and fur of coats turns to the needles of spruce and pine
and the smell of mothballs becomes the smell of the cold
there where it's always winter but never Christmas.
There are places one can only reach by turning sideways,
  closing one's eyes,
and slipping between the dreams as if between cool sheets.
There's the Shire, where every county's a Farthing,
somewhere between the Grey Havens and Rivendell,
where each door is round
and gives on the ground,
and Arkham, split by the dream-haunted Miskatonic,
west of Hangman's Hill and somewhat south of the Dark Ravine
and above the lairs of Nyarlahotep, the Goat with a Thousand Young.
    At times they cross pollinate, you know,

One of Stephen's professors advised him that the best way to get a book published was to write about something current, like the war in Vietnam.[11] Stephen began working on *Sword in the Darkness*, about a gang of crooks who plan to start a race riot at an urban high school as a distraction while they rob several criminal enterprises. The professor worked on the first half of the book with Stephen, one chapter at a time. Stephen sent the partial manuscript to a publisher and received the exact response the professor had warned him he would get: a request to get back in touch when the book was finished. Ultimately, *Sword in the Darkness*, which was approximately 150,000 words, earned a dozen rejections and remains unpublished to this day (except for one chapter that was included in *Stephen King: Uncollected and Unpublished*,[12] where the novel is described in detail).

During his first two years at college, Stephen wrote short stories for *Ubris*, the University of Maine's literary magazine. (Copies of these rare publications now often sell to collectors for hundreds of dollars.) He also made a second sale to *Startling Mystery Stories* in 1969 with the story "The Reaper's Image."

In January 1969, Stephen wrote a letter to the *Maine Campus*. In it, he criticized the paper for its lack of coverage on issues of the day. An editor at the paper responded with, "We could use people like you." So less than a month later, Stephen started contributing a regular column called "King's Garbage Truck" in which he wrote about politics (local and global), movies, music, books, and sports. Although Stephen struggled financially while at the University of Maine, academically he excelled. He ended up on the deans' list in 1969 and supported himself that summer with a work-study job at the university library. There he met Tabitha Spruce at a picnic for library employees. Stephen says that it was her raucous, wonderful, and unafraid laugh that first caught his attention. He says he fell in love with her during a poetry workshop class (he was a senior; she was a junior). He was impressed by the poetry she presented and how she understood what she was doing with her work.

In 1969, Stephen wrote a one-act play called *The Accident*, which won the English Department's Hamlet Award. He was publishing in university journals and receiving encouragement from university faculty. However, he was still several years away from becoming a successful writer who could support himself and the family he would soon be starting.

OPPOSITE LEFT: *Startling Mystery Stories* (1967) containing "The Glass Floor," King's first professional sale. OPPOSITE RIGHT: *Moth* (1970), an off-campus publication containing three poems by King: "The Dark Man," "Donovan's Brain," and "Silence."

Fall No. 6

CME

STARTLING MYSTERY STORIES

50c

UNUSUAL - EERIE - STRANGE

MOTH

CHAPTER 2

THE DOUBLEDAY YEARS (1970s)

Everything changed for Stephen King in the 1970s. In the 1960s he was a struggling, single college student. By the end of the seventies, he would be married with three children and was, at last, a published novelist and rising star in the world of horror fiction. Even so, Stephen and his family had a lot to endure before he became an "overnight success."

King at Hampden Academy.

Stephen found the incomplete manuscript of *Getting It On* in a box in the cellar of the house where he grew up and finished the novel in 1971. He sent the manuscript to the publisher Doubleday, where it ended up on the desk of an editor named Bill Thompson. Bill thought the manuscript was masterfully written, but no one else at Doubleday was as excited about it. Bill requested three rewrites from Stephen, but was ultimately forced to pass on it. Stephen's novel *The Long Walk* met with a similar fate.

Stephen King and Tabitha Spruce were married in 1971. Stephen wore a borrowed suit that was too large for him to the ceremony. Their daughter, Naomi, had been born the previous year. Unable to find a teaching position, Stephen took a low-paying job at the New Franklin Laundry, and Tabitha worked at Dunkin' Donuts.

Their combined income was barely enough to support them. Any unexpected expenses stretched their budget past its breaking point. During those lean times, Stephen recalls that on-publication checks for the short stories he was submitting to magazines would arrive to save the day.

In the fall of 1971, Stephen landed a teaching job at the Hampden Academy in Maine. The starting salary of $6,400 a year seemed like a huge jump from his minimum-wage hourly pay at the laundry. However, the amount of extracurricular work involved at the school ate into his writing time. "By most Friday afternoons I felt as if I'd spent the week with jumper cables clamped to my brain," he recalls.[13] During summer break in 1972, when their son Joseph was born, Stephen once again worked at the industrial laundry company.

Still struggling financially, the family lived in a rented mobile home. One day, when Stephen arrived home from work, Tabitha made him hand over all his credit cards. She cut them into pieces, and they lived without credit cards for the next two years. Stephen wrote another novel, *The Running Man*, in less than a week during spring break in 1972. However, Bill Thompson wasn't interested in the book.

EDITOR BILL THOMPSON

Editor Bill Thompson is credited with discovering two famous authors: Stephen King and John Grisham. Bill's encouragement kept Stephen writing, even after several novels had been rejected. However, Bill knew *Carrie* was the charm.

The publisher had approved an advance of $1,500. Bill bumped it up to $2,500 and sneaked it past the accountants and contract department. He edited Stephen's next four books. When Stephen decided to end his relationship with Doubleday at the end of the 1970s, Bill was let go by the publisher, but Bill and Stephen remained close over the years, and they worked together again when Stephen wrote *Danse Macabre*.

CARRIE (1974)

Unable to come up with a new idea, Stephen revisited a short story he had started the previous year. The tale of a bullied teenage girl with telekinetic powers was a response to a friend's challenge to write from a female point of view. Hoping for something that would earn him a quick paycheck from a magazine, Stephen stopped working on it when he realized the story needed a "longer fuse before the explosion."[14] In other words, it felt like a novel, and he didn't think he had the time it would take to finish one. Stephen also felt he didn't know enough about teenage girls to write the story.

He threw the four single-spaced pages in the trash, but Tabby rescued them and encouraged him to finish the novel that would become *Carrie*. She also helped in other ways. "Tabby was able to supply doorways at crucial moments," Stephen recalled in an interview.[15]

The first draft was less than a hundred pages—too long to be published as a short story and too short for a novel. Stephen decided to expand it by adding fake news articles and new scenes. He finished revising the manuscript, ending up with a short novel. Still, he had so little faith in it, and felt so dejected by his experiences with Doubleday, that he decided not to send it to Bill Thompson. There didn't seem to be much of a market for horror novels at the time. When Bill later sent Stephen a country music calendar, Stephen decided to submit *Carrie*.

After a round of revisions, Bill told Stephen he was cautiously optimistic Doubleday would publish *Carrie*.

Doubleday hardcover edition of *Carrie*.

CARRIE

STEPHEN KING

Doubleday & Company, Inc.
GARDEN CITY, NEW YORK
1974

This is for Tabby, who got me into it—and then bailed me
out of it.

ABOVE: Author photo for *Carrie*. INSET TOP: Cover
page. INSET BOTTOM: Dedication page. King's original
text read "This is for Tabby, who forced me into it."

Encouraged, Stephen borrowed $75 from his wife's grandmother for an all-night bus ride from Maine to New York City to meet his editor for the first time.

A month later, Doubleday purchased the novel. Word of the sale came by telegram since the Kings had gotten rid of their telephone to save money.

The advance, although respectable for a first novel in 1973, was barely enough to buy a new car to replace their old vehicle, which had just lost its transmission. It certainly wasn't enough for Stephen to give up his teaching job.

Then, on Mother's Day 1973, he received a life-changing phone call (by now the Kings had a phone again). Doubleday had sold the rights for the paperback edition of *Carrie* to Signet Books for $400,000. (That's over $2.79 million in today's dollars.) Stephen would get half of that and Doubleday would get the rest. This meant he could finally quit his day job and write full-time. However, if Stephen turned out to be a one-hit wonder, that money—although it was far more than he had ever seen in his life—wouldn't last forever.

However, it did mean Stephen could do something for his mother, who had supported him all his life and was now battling cancer. "My brother and I . . . went to the Pineland facility where she worked. And my brother and I, we said, 'Mom, you're done. There's enough to take care of you now, because the book sold for a lot of money, and you can go home.'"[16]

Ruth King died at the age of sixty, before *Carrie* was published. However, she must have gained some satisfaction from knowing that her son was finally a published novelist.

'SALEM'S LOT (1975)

Stephen first read *Dracula* when he was eleven, then he rediscovered the book almost fifteen years later when he was teaching a high school course called Fantasy and Science Fiction. Over dinner one night with Tabitha and childhood friend Chris Chesley, the conversation turned to how differently things might have gone if Dracula had come to America in the 1970s instead of turn-of-the-century London. What if, instead of a big city, Dracula landed in rural Maine, a place so isolated that almost anything could happen there? Stephen thought, "People could drop out of sight, disappear, perhaps even come back as the living dead."[17] He felt a contemporary setting would work in a vampire's favor because modern conveniences would make it hard for people to believe in his existence.

Stephen started writing *Second Coming* in 1972, when life was still difficult for the family. He wrote in the furnace room of their trailer with a fourth-grade desk propped on his knees to support his wife's typewriter, while Tabitha tried to figure out which bills had to be paid now and which could be put off. Fighting vampires was a form of escape for Stephen. They seemed less threatening than the debt collectors harassing the family. He finished the first draft the day before he received the call from Thompson about the paperback jackpot from *Carrie*.

As a follow-up to *Carrie*, Stephen gave Bill Thompson two manuscripts to consider: *Roadwork*, later published as a Richard Bachman novel, and *Second Coming* (later retitled *'Salem's Lot*). Bill warned Stephen that if they went with the vampire novel, Stephen ran the risk of being pigeonholed as a horror writer. Stephen thought about all the horror writers whose work he'd enjoyed over the years. "I'll be a horror writer if that's what people want. That's just fine," he responded.[18]

Although vampires have become common in contemporary horror, Stephen is credited with ditching their traditional Gothic settings. In one fell swoop, he both modernized and Americanized horror. *'Salem's Lot* sold about 26,000 copies in hardcover and the paperback edition earned an advance of $500,000 (again, split with Doubleday). When it became his first bestseller, Stephen's future as a full-time writer seemed certain at last.

Title page from King's first draft of *'Salem's Lot*.

THE SHINING (1977)

On a whim, the Kings moved to Boulder, Colorado, in 1974. Stephen wanted to write a book set somewhere other than Maine. A finger stab at a map of the United States determined their destination, according to one version of the story. They drove west and moved the family into a rented house.

That fall, Stephen and Tabitha left their two children with a babysitter for a weekend getaway at the Stanley Hotel in Estes Park, forty miles north of Boulder. They arrived the night before the hotel closed for the winter and were its only guests. The dining room was still open, but only one meal was being served. The chairs were turned upside down atop every table except theirs, and the tuxedo-clad orchestra played for them and them alone.

The empty hotel struck Stephen as the perfect setting for a ghost story. After Tabitha went to bed, Stephen wandered the deserted halls. He encountered many of *The Shining*'s iconic images, including a bartender named Grady and a clawfoot bathtub that looked like someone could die in it—or already had. Later, he dreamed of his three-year-old son, Joe, screaming as a fire hose chased him down the hotel's endless hallways. By the end of the night, Stephen had the story outline mapped out in his head.

For years, Stephen had been toying with an idea about a boy with the power to make dreams become real. That novel, which was to be called *Darkshine*, was set in an amusement park. However, Stephen couldn't come up with a logical reason why the characters wouldn't simply flee from the park screaming for help once bad things started to happen. A snowbound hotel solved that problem.

The book developed from a combination of several ideas; the visit to the Stanley Hotel simply helped bring them all together. Stephen was also inspired by other books and stories he'd read, including "The Veldt" by Ray Bradbury, "The Fall of the House of Usher" and "The Masque of the Red Death" by Edgar Allan Poe, and *The Haunting of Hill House* by Shirley Jackson.

Since their rental house was rather small, Stephen leased office space in a boarding house where he could look out the window at the Flatiron Mountains. He remembers that once he started working on the book, he entered a zone where everything he wrote worked: "The story unspooled itself without a hitch or a snag. I never had that depressing feeling that I had lost my way."[19] He averaged 3,000 words per day, and the first draft required the least rewriting of all of his early books. Stephen felt himself "mesmerized by the story."[20]

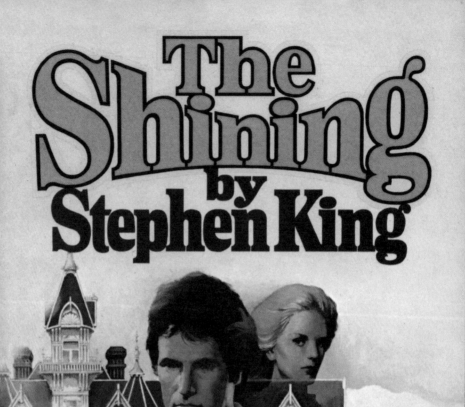

The Shining
by
Stephen King

A new novel
by the
author of
CARRIE
and
'SALEM'S LOT

Although the writing came fast, the process of putting into words the story of a man isolated with his family drew Stephen back to his days of poverty. "For much of the three or four months it took me to write the first draft," he recalls, "I seemed to be back in that trailer in Hermon, Maine, with no company but the buzzing sound of the snowmobiles and my own fears—fears that my chance to be a writer had come and gone, fears that I had gotten into a teaching job that was completely wrong for me, fears most of all that my marriage was edging onto marshy ground and that there might be quicksand anyplace ahead."[21]

Stephen was already a heavy drinker by this point. Struggling to support his family while trying to break through as a writer had taken its toll, as had his mother's death. In interviews, he confessed to feeling rage toward his family—and guilt over the anger—but he didn't make a direct connection between himself and the father in *The Shining* until after he became sober. "By making Jack Torrance a drinker . . . I found myself able to look around a dark corner and to see myself as I could have been, under the right set of circumstances."[22] Fifteen years after that visit to the Stanley Hotel, Stephen wrote about his revelation one night, "I'm an alcoholic, I thought . . . I was, after all, the guy who had written *The Shining* without even realizing (at least until that night) that I was writing about myself."[23]

Like the Kings, the Torrance family flees to Colorado from New England. However, the reason for the Torrances' move is very different than the Kings'. Jack Torrance is desperate. He's unemployed, his writing isn't going anywhere, his five-year-old son, Danny, is having emotional problems, and his wife, Wendy, has had enough. Taking a job as the winter caretaker of the Overlook Hotel is one of the few straws left for Jack to grasp.

Jack sees his potential as a "blooming American writer" slipping away. Teaching was leaving him little time to write, a situation Stephen was quite familiar with. Jack intends to spend his snowbound months in the empty hotel finishing a play called *The Little School*. Wendy is happy he is writing again, thinking he "seemed to be slowly closing a huge door on a roomful of monsters." She has no idea what is in store for them in the Overlook.

In the grand Gothic tradition, the Overlook Hotel is a bad place. Stephen saw it as "a huge storage battery charged with an evil powerful enough to corrupt all those who

OPPOSITE: Doubleday hardcover edition of *The Shining*.

come into contact with it."[24] The evil derives from a century of horrific incidents that have taken place within its walls. In *The Shining*'s introduction, he asks the reader, "Aren't memories the true ghosts of our lives? Do they not drive us all to words and acts we regret from time to time?"[25]

Jack's weak character makes him vulnerable to the hotel's evil. It is an open question whether he would have survived the winter trapped with his family even without the evil influence of the Overlook. All he needs is one more bad thing to happen to push him over the edge. In the introduction, Stephen says, "I believe these [horror] stories exist because we sometimes need to create unreal monsters and bogies to stand in for all the things we fear in our real lives."[26]

Stephen's hope, though, is that "you don't get scared of monsters—you get scared for people."[27] This sums up one of the secrets of his success—his books are about how people react to stressful circumstances. He makes readers care for his characters and then throws something catastrophic at them.

Stephen considers Jack a fundamentally good person who succumbs to the terrible attraction of violence.[28] "Jack Torrance himself is a haunted house," Stephen says. "He's haunted by his father."[29] It's not surprising that Stephen has mixed feelings toward fathers, given the fact that his own had abandoned the family when he was two. He later reflected in an interview, "I was encountering fatherhood from my end and I'd never experienced it from any other end—that is, being a child and having a father and going on fishing trips and all the rest of that stuff."[30] Though Jack seems to be the hotel's main target, its real goal is Jack's son, Danny, who has extrasensory powers. Wendy is a strong, independent woman (unlike the way she is depicted in Stanley Kubrick's film adaptation). She is trapped in a haunted hotel, miles from civilization, with a man undergoing a breakdown. However, she doesn't surrender the way Jack does. Her determination to survive and resist the evils, both natural and supernatural, allows her and Danny to make it out alive against terrible odds.

Stephen structured the book like a five-act Shakespearean play. The first draft had scenes instead of chapters and ended with Wendy and Danny escaping from the hotel on a snowmobile with Dick Halloran, the head chef at the hotel who returned after receiving a psychic summons from Danny. Feeling there were too many loose ends, Stephen added a prologue that detailed the hotel's checkered past and an epilogue.

As a cost-saving measure, Doubleday removed the prologue and most of the epilogue. The prologue was published in *Whispers* magazine in 1982 and was later

THE STANLEY HOTEL

F. O. Stanley, inventor of the Stanley Steamer automobile, built the Stanley Hotel between 1907 and 1909. Unlike *The Shining*'s Overlook Hotel, though, the Stanley is not isolated. It is perched on a hillside above the town of Estes Park, Colorado.

When it came time to remake the novel as a miniseries for television in 1997, Stephen and director Mick Garris decided to film on location. The production team restored sections of the hotel to their original glory as part of the deal that allowed them to use the site. To create the illusion of isolation, digital effects were used to remove any other buildings that made it into camera range.

Stephen's novel and its adaptations have raised the hotel's profile as a haunted destination. Teams of ghost hunters have filmed their paranormal investigations, declaring the hotel the second-most haunted in the United States. Most of the activity is said to take place on the fourth floor, two stories above the famous room 217.

The owners are quick to explain that any supernatural presences belong to "good spirits." One of the ghosts is supposed to be Lord Dunraven, who sold the land for the hotel to Stanley. However, Dunraven left Colorado in the 1880s, so how his ghost ended up back there is anyone's guess.

The hotel featured in Stanley Kubrick's 1980 film adaptation was a combination of exteriors shot at the Timberline Lodge in Mount Hood, Oregon, and interiors and a facade constructed on a sound stage in England.

The Stanley Hotel in Estes Park, Colorado, King's inspiration for the Overlook Hotel.

LEFT: A Doubleday promotional photo of Stephen, circa 1975, by Alex Gotfyrd. OPPOSITE: The Torrance family escapes to Colorado in Stanley Kubrick's film adaptation of *The Shining*. Shelly Duvall as Wendy, Danny Lloyd as Danny, and Jack Nicholson as Jack Torrance. INSET: A promotional doorplate from *The Shining* miniseries.

abridged in *TV Guide* when the miniseries adaptation aired on ABC in 1997. The prologue and the recently rediscovered epilogue were both included in the deluxe edition of the novel published by Cemetery Dance in 2017.

Stephen's original title for the book, *The Shine*, came from John Lennon's song "Instant Karma," but Doubleday changed it because "shine" was thought to be a negative term. Stephen said he could live with the new title but found it "rather unwieldy and thudding."[31] However, the success of *The Shining* inspired countless horror novels with titles consisting of "The" followed by a word ending in "-ing," used by authors and publishers hoping to strike the same winning chord as *The Shining*.

The book was a hit. *The Shining* landed on the *New York Times* bestseller list and sold tens of thousands of copies. Five years later, copies were selling on the rare book market for over $200. The book has come to be seen as a modern classic for which Stephen King will probably be remembered for generations.

STEPHEN KING AS RICHARD BACHMAN

RAGE (1977), *THE LONG WALK* (1979), *ROADWORK* (1981), *THE RUNNING MAN* (1982)

After he had published a few books and developed name recognition, Stephen asked Doubleday if they would publish some of his earlier novels. Doubleday didn't want to flood the market, though. At the time, there was a belief in publishing that there was a limit to how many books by a given author readers were willing to buy each year. New books hurt the sales of older books, according to this theory.

Therefore, Stephen sent *Getting It On*—the book Bill Thompson had worked so hard to get published—to Elaine Koster, his editor at New American Library (NAL), the company that had purchased the paperback rights to his novels for huge amounts of money. They planned to publish *Getting It On* under a pen name to see if it would find its own audience without Stephen's name on the cover. Stephen wanted to use Guy Pillsbury, his grandfather's name, as his pseudonym. However, this alias was accidentally revealed internally at NAL, so he was pressed to come up with a new one quickly.

"There was a novel by Richard Stark on my desk so I used the name Richard . . . and what was playing on the record player was 'You Ain't Seen Nothin' Yet' by Bachman-Turner Overdrive, so I put the two of them together and came up with Richard Bachman."[32]

The book had to get a new title, too: *Rage*. It was published as a $1.50 mass-market paperback in 1977, eight months after *The Shining*. It received one lackluster review and was only available at book racks at drugstores and bus stations.[33] Novels like these had short lifespans—a couple of months at most and they were gone.

Would Stephen's career have been different if Doubleday had published *Getting It On* first instead of *Carrie*? Perhaps a little, Stephen says, but "in the long run, the monster would have come out."[34]

Between 1977 and 1982, Richard Bachman published three more books: *The Long Walk* (1979), *Roadwork* (1981), and *The Running Man* (1982). Several people claimed that Richard Bachman was in fact Stephen King, but Stephen always denied the rumors.

When *Thinner*, by Richard Bachman, came out in hardcover in 1984, one reviewer declared this was what Stephen King would write like if Stephen King could write. Other reviewers noticed the similarity in style, and the fake author photo and bio on the dust jacket didn't dampen their suspicions. A resourceful bookstore employee named Stephen P. Brown researched the copyrights for the previous four Bachman novels at the Library of Congress. There he found the proof that the books were written by Stephen King. Sales of *Thinner*, already more impressive than for any of the previous Bachman books, skyrocketed after the news broke. Richard Bachman died of "exposure" (later upgraded to "cancer of the pseudonym") after his identity was exposed.

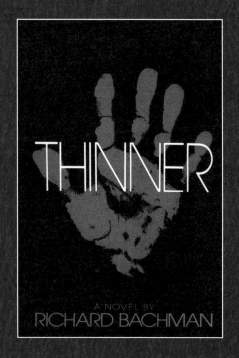

New American Library first edition of *Thinner*, King's fifth novel published under the pen name Richard Bachman—and the first in hardcover.

NIGHT SHIFT (1978)

"Jerusalem's Lot," "Graveyard Shift," "Night Surf," "I Am the Doorway," "The Mangler," "The Boogeyman," "Gray Matter," "Battleground," "Trucks," "Sometimes They Come Back," "Strawberry Spring," "The Ledge," "The Lawnmower Man," "Quitters, Inc.," "I Know What You Need," "Children of the Corn," "The Last Rung on the Ladder," "The Man Who Loved Flowers," "One for the Road," "The Woman in the Room"

Although Doubleday didn't want to publish more than one book by Stephen King a year, they still wanted no less than a book a year from him. While working on what would become one of his longest novels, *The Stand*, Stephen realized it wouldn't be finished to meet Doubleday's schedule. To bridge the gap, he offered them a short story collection.

Night Shift consists of sixteen stories published between 1968 and 1977, along with four previously unpublished stories. Bill Thompson helped Stephen pick the best of the available material for this collection. The book includes a foreword by Stephen that discusses the nature of fear and our fascination with it—about why people read horror fiction and why he writes it.

Doubleday wasn't optimistic about the collection. The first printing was smaller than for *'Salem's Lot*. However, *Night Shift* proved to be so popular that Doubleday had to issue a second printing within weeks of publication. It sold around 24,000 copies in the first year, a very respectable number for a collection.

THE STAND (1978)

Stephen's 1969 short story "Night Surf" was published in the University of Maine literary magazine *Ubris* and extensively reworked before he resold it to *Cavalier* magazine in 1974. It is about a group of teenagers who survived a virus called A6 that wiped out most of mankind. The teenagers believe they are immune, but as the story develops, some begin to show symptoms of the disease, which they call "Captain Trips." Stephen wanted to tell a longer story about the world after the virus, but he didn't feel ready to write it at that time.

After he finished *The Shining*, he wrote the novella *Apt Pupil*, then spent six weeks working on another novel, but it wasn't coming together for him. Then he read about an accident in Utah where canisters of a deadly chemical fell from a truck, split open, and killed some sheep. The news accounts hinted that, if the wind had been blowing in a different direction, a toxic cloud might have threatened Salt Lake City. A short while later, the first ever outbreak of Legionnaires' disease occurred in Philadelphia. When he heard a radio preacher utter the phrase, "once in every generation, the plague will fall among them," he liked it enough to write it down and post it on his desk.

Stephen finally gave up on the book he was working on and started a two-year trek across America with the survivors of the superflu. Writing an epic fantasy with a host of characters—some good, some evil—on the scale of *The Lord of the Rings* appealed to Stephen. Readers wouldn't need to learn a fantasy language or require maps of a fictitious landscape. The setting would be eerily familiar already—the United States.

DOLLAR BABIES

In the 1980s, Frank Darabont, a film director, screenwriter, and producer, acquired the rights to adapt Stephen's *Night Shift* short story "The Woman in the Room," for just $1. This was one of the first of a series of projects that became known as "Dollar Babies." (Darabont would go on to write and direct the films *The Shawshank Redemption*, *The Green Mile*, and *The Mist*.)

Stephen had a few conditions when he granted limited, one-time rights to young filmmakers to adapt a short story where the film rights were still available: "I ask them to sign a paper promising that no resulting film will be exhibited commercially without approval, and that they send me a videotape of the finished work."[35] This meant they could only be shown at film festivals or other venues where admission was free, and they couldn't be posted on the internet.

Several of Stephen's short stories were filmed numerous times by different directors. However, once Stephen sold commercial movie rights to a story, it was no longer available under this program. The films vary widely in quality, style, and approach. Some are animated, although most are live-action. A few have been adapted into foreign languages. Stephen typically was not involved with these productions, although he did contribute a voice cameo to an adaptation of "Lunch at the Gotham Café."

Stephen ended the "Dollar Baby" program in December 2023 when the person who had been handling the contracts retired.

TOP: Goya's painting *Duel With Clubs*, which likely inspired the artwork for the cover of *The Stand*. BOTTOM: Doubleday first edition hardcover.

THE STAND
a novel by the author of
THE SHINING
STEPHEN KING

He approached the project with glee. He saw the superflu as an unusual solution to the energy crisis. People wouldn't have to line up at gas stations any longer. The Cold War would end, pollution would lessen, and the planet would get a breather. There was a chance for the world to start over again.

At first, Stephen started the book from one character's perspective as she gathers followers on a trek across the ravaged landscape of the former America, like Dorothy in *The Wizard of Oz*. This approach proved clunky, though, so instead Stephen opted to write the novel from multiple viewpoints. The ordeals of the survivors are told in separate chapters until they all get together in the west.

The first section of the novel is devoted to the way the Captain Trips virus spreads across the country, killing almost everyone in its wake. However, Stephen was more interested in what would happen afterward. In his mind, an idealist group would focus on recreating society and reestablishing fundamental rights, while people happy to be free from the rule of law would start stockpiling weapons for a conflict both sides realized was inevitable.

He explained once in an interview, "If almost everybody died, think of everything that would be left around . . . nuclear weapons and things like that. You could have a society in Schenectady and another one in a place like Boston, and they could get into a theological argument and end up literally exchanging nuclear weapons. I mean, those things are not that hard to run. . . . Might take them a little while, but it wouldn't take them very long."[36]

The Stand is about more than survival, though. The survivors are presented with a moral dilemma: Are they fundamentally good or evil? Do they respond to the summons of the benign Mother Abigail or to that of the dark man, Randall Flagg, the Walkin' Dude? Do they join the Boulder Free Zone or go to Las Vegas, a city Stephen thinks of as fundamentally bland, which even today is sometimes referred to as Sin City?

Writing this epic novel was hard work for Stephen. "I kept telling myself that in another hundred pages or so, I would begin to see light at the end of the tunnel," he remembered.[37] Then he experienced a profound case of writer's block after 500 pages. Using a familiar baseball metaphor, he says the book "nearly died going into the third turn and heading for home."[38] If he had spent less time on it, he might have abandoned it. "There were times when I actively hated *The Stand*, but there was never a time when I did not feel compelled to go on with it."[39]

He started taking long walks ("a habit which would, two decades later, get me in a lot of trouble"[40]) as he tried to sort out the complex maze of plots and characters. After struggling with this problem for several weeks, the solution came to him. He had depopulated the world, but his book was becoming overcrowded with characters again. Some of them had to go.

Stephen wrote the rest of the novel in a little over two months, ending up with a 1,400-plus-page manuscript. Although he trimmed it during revision, Doubleday insisted he cut the manuscript significantly before they would publish it. They believed the book was going to be too expensive, which would hurt sales. Stephen was presented with two options: either he could axe 400 pages or someone at Doubleday would. This was the second time Stephen had been asked to remove material for purely economic reasons. He wasn't happy about it, but he did it. (This demand added to his growing list of grievances with Doubleday, though, and probably contributed to his move to a new publisher for future novels.)

The Stand almost always appears in first or second place in polls asking fans to name their favorite Stephen King novel. "There are people out there who would have been perfectly happy had I died in 1978, the people who come to me and say, 'Oh, you never wrote a book as good as *The Stand*.' I usually tell them how depressing it is to hear them say that something you wrote . . . years ago was your best book."[41]

THE DEAD ZONE (1979)

The Shining and *The Stand* both end with characters moving to Maine. In the summer of 1975, while Stephen was still working on the first draft of *The Stand*, he and his family did the same. He didn't feel like he belonged in Boulder, recognizing that his characters all had a Maine working-class sensibility.

After finishing *The Stand*, he struggled to complete another novel, abandoning two before starting a book about a killer in a small town. "The germ of *The Dead Zone* never really made it into the novel. . . . I wanted to write about a high school teacher, because that was a profession I knew quite well but I had never used in a novel. I saw him giving an examination to his class—it becomes very quiet, everyone's head is bent over their papers, and a girl comes up and hands him the test. Their hands touch, and he says into this quiet: 'You must go home at once, your house is on fire.' And I could see everyone in the room looking at him—all the eyes, staring."[42]

THE **Park Lane Hotel** 36 CENTRAL PARK SOUTH, NEW YORK, N.Y. 10019 (212) 371 - 4000

May 22, 1978.

Concerning the copy-edited MS. of _The Stand_:

1.) when characters drop g's in their dialogue (and in a few cases, when g's are dropped in narration), I have ~~omitted~~ omitted the customary apostrophe which usually denotes the missing letter. I would like to see this convention followed when setting the book in type. Same applies to the short form of "them" —em. Also: rock n roll, and o for the short form of "of" (as in: "Hand me that pad o paper, Nick.")

2.) Instead of U.S. 95 or U.S. 6, (etc.) please set US in all cases, as indicated.

Thank you very much,

Stephen King

A drive-in marquee in Indianapolis, announcing a King movie marathon in 1984.

When he had problems turning that idea into a novel, Stephen put the manuscript aside and began *Firestarter*. "I felt slightly desperate to finish something, and I think that, subconsciously, I returned to what I had written before."[43] Concerned he was simply reworking *Carrie*, he went back to *The Dead Zone*, completing the novel in 1977.

Stephen describes how the main character's supernatural power developed in his mind: "Little by little [Johnny Smith's ability] refined itself into this psychic talent that's known as 'prolepsis.'. . . It's the ability to be sort of a human bloodhound—to touch objects and get visions from them. . . . Everybody would sort of shun him as a result of this. Everybody would be afraid of him. . . . The more I wrote, the more it seemed like just a really horrible thing, you know? People wouldn't like you."[44]

Stephen's move to Maine was only one of several life changes during this time. He engaged the services of a literary agent for the first time, and he cut his ties with Doubleday. Agent Kirby McCauley negotiated a $2.5 million advance with NAL—the publisher of the paperback editions of his books—for three novels: *The Dead Zone*, *Firestarter*, and another unspecified book. This was a huge improvement over the rather small advances Stephen had received in the past for the hardcover editions. This deal also meant he would no longer have to split the profits from the paperback rights with the publisher. In a reversal of the normal procedure at the time, NAL subsequently searched for a hardcover deal for *The Dead Zone*. Numerous publishers turned it down because the book was so different from what Stephen was known for. Ultimately, editor Alan Williams at Viking agreed to take a chance on the book.

The Dead Zone is set primarily in Cleaves Mills, Maine, which is close to Castle Rock, one of Stephen's most famous fictional locations, appearing for the first time in this book. The town's name is taken from William Golding's novel *Lord of the Flies*, which had a major influence on Stephen's work.

The main character, Johnny Smith, becomes psychic after two accidents. The first takes place on a frozen pond when he is six. An older boy accidentally knocks him down and his head hits the ice, reflecting an incident from Stephen's childhood when he was knocked out after colliding with a hockey player. The second incident happens when Johnny is twenty-three at a time in his life when everything appears to be going

King on July 4, 1952. He was knocked unconscious by a hockey player when he was four, an incident that found its way into *The Dead Zone*.

his way. He's a high school teacher and has a girlfriend he seems destined to marry. Then, on the drive home after a date, he is involved in a car accident that leaves him in a coma for over five years.

Although Stephen's previous novels featured evil personified—vampires, the ghosts in a haunted hotel, the diabolical Randall Flagg—the evil in *The Dead Zone* is more abstract. What happens to Johnny is a random act. His decision not to spend the night with his girlfriend after eating a bad hot dog put him on a collision course with fate. Stephen explains, "To me, everything that's symbolic in *The Dead Zone* points in one direction. It seems as though our lives are governed by these little 'chance' events. If you draw back and take a longer view, maybe there's a pattern to it all. I like to think there is; I'd hate to think that life is all random."[45]

Brooke Adams as Sarah Bracknell and Martin Sheen as Greg Stillson in the 1983 adaptation of *The Dead Zone*.

Johnny emerges from his lengthy coma to discover that the bulk of his twenties have been stolen from him. His girlfriend is now married to another man and has a son. His memories are full of "dead zones," things he can't recall. To make matters worse, he has visions of the future, and most of them aren't pleasant.

The media is drawn to Johnny's story. He becomes a minor celebrity, and people start demanding his help. Journalists stalk him. When he becomes overwhelmed by all the requests, he withdraws from society. It is tempting to think Stephen was reflecting on the difficulties he was having adjusting to his own loss of privacy because of his newfound celebrity. By this point, strangers were constantly requesting autographs, money, or contacts in the publishing industry.

However, Johnny reluctantly accepts one plea for assistance. He agrees to help Sheriff George Bannerman solve a series of murders in nearby Castle Rock and quickly identifies one of Bannerman's deputies, Frank Dodd, as the killer. There's nothing supernatural about Dodd's murders, although his spirit would later be invoked as a monster who haunts Castle Rock in *Cujo*.

The Dead Zone gets down to its primary business, however, when it tackles the subject of Greg Stillson, the corrupt politician who once kicked a dog to death when he was a Bible salesman. According to one of Johnny's visions, Stillson will one day become president of the United States and start a full-scale nuclear war. By this point, Johnny has enough experience with his visions to trust what he foresees. He is presented with a moral conundrum: Is he obligated to do something to prevent this future catastrophe? If he decides to kill Stillson, would he be justified?

Stephen states, "*The Dead Zone* arose from two questions: Can a political assassin ever be right? And if he is, could you make him the protagonist of a novel?"[46] Or, in other words, "Would you kill Hitler if you could go back in a time machine?"[47] Stephen uses the fact that readers know about Stillson's true nature to generate their support for Johnny's actions. He does indeed become a sympathetic would-be assassin. As Stephen says, "Johnny is different from other violent, paranoid mystics in only one way: He really can see the future."[48]

Stephen casts Johnny as a genuinely decent guy—his name is the epitome of average—and ultimately shies away from having Johnny kill Stillson. "Part of me said, you don't want to do this because if he kills Greg Stillson in the book, and ten years from now somebody knocks off . . . President Carter, and they ask him, 'Why did you do it?' The guy says, 'I got the idea from Stephen King's novel *The Dead Zone*,' I would have to quietly pack my bags and move to Costa Rica. So, I was ambivalent. A lot of me wanted to kill [Stillson] and felt the ending was something of a cop-out."[49]

Stephen calls *The Dead Zone* "plot-driven," meaning the characters of his protagonist and antagonist were determined by the story he wanted to tell. It remains one of his personal favorites. Thanks in part to an attractively designed book cover and an aggressive marketing campaign, *The Dead Zone* became Stephen's first number one hardcover bestseller, and it stayed on the list for nearly half a year.

ADAPTATIONS

There was strong interest in making a movie from *Carrie* before it was published, but no one wanted to put up a lot of money to option the film rights to the book. Doubleday decided to wait until after the novel came out, gambling on it becoming a bestseller, which would increase interest in the movie rights. Even though *Carrie* didn't do well in hardcover, movie rights were sold for $2,500 soon after it was published.

Stephen was asked who his top choice would be for a director. He named Brian De Palma on the strength of one of his earlier movies. After shopping the project around, it ended up at United Artists with a budget of less than $2 million.

Although the producer, Paul Monash, wasn't convinced De Palma was right for the film, he understood the studio wanted him as director, so he agreed. When the movie was released in 1976, it grossed nearly $34 million at the box office and inspired over a million people to buy the paperback edition. It also garnered Academy Award nominations for Sissy Spacek and Piper Laurie, providing a big boost to Stephen's writing career, as well as to De Palma's directing career.

OPPOSITE: Piper Laurie, holding her daughter (Sissy Spacek), in her Oscar-nominated role as Margaret White in *Carrie*, 1976. ABOVE: Reggie Nalder as the vampire Barlow in the 1979 miniseries *'Salem's Lot*, menacing Mark Petrie, played by Lance Kerwin.

Warner Bros optioned *'Salem's Lot* "for a lot of money"[50] before the novel was published. De Palma's adaptation of *Carrie* hadn't been released yet, so it was a gamble. The original plan was to make a feature film from the book, but after numerous scripts and years in development, the studio finally decided to make a four-hour TV miniseries for CBS. Monash was hired to write the script. The $4-million adaptation aired on two consecutive Saturday evenings in November 1979. The teleplay was nominated for an Edgar Award and the miniseries earned several technical Emmy nominations.

See Appendix II for an extensive list of adaptations.

WELCOME TO CASTLE ROCK

The fictional Maine town of Castle Rock has figured prominently in Stephen's books and stories. "I like that town," Stephen says. "I know where a lot of stuff is in that town. I don't have any maps. I don't have all the names categorized, but I like that town."[51]

Castle Rock is a little mill town in the Lakes Region of western Maine, not far from the New Hampshire border. It's located ninety miles from Portland, and sixty-five miles from Jerusalem's Lot (although Stephen once said, "Castle Rock is really just Jerusalem's Lot without the vampires"[52]). A sign on the outskirts of town says that Castle Rock is a nice place to live and grow.

Its 2,000 residents are divided among those who are From Town and those who are From Away. The founders made full use of the Castle name. Castle View is right next door. Nearby bodies of water are the Castle Stream, Castle River, and Castle Lake. The wealthier people live on Castle Hill.

Above the town is Castle View, which can be reached by taking Route 117 (View Drive) or Pleasant Road. Once upon a time, you could also climb the so-called

"Suicide Stairs," a staircase containing 305 zigzag steps up the cliffside to the viewing platform at the top, but they were destroyed by a mysterious tremor in 1979. From the top, you can see the entire town below and, to the west, forests, lakes, and mountains all the way to Vermont and New Hampshire.

What makes Castle Rock stand out from all the other little towns in the state is the fact that a lot of bad things happen there. In 1911, a farmer chopped up his wife and kids and then said in court that ghosts made him do it. Between 1970 and 1975, six females between the ages of nine and seventy-one were murdered by the Castle Rock Strangler (a.k.a. the November Killer), who turned out to be one of the county's deputies, Frank Dodd. Dodd ultimately died by suicide after being exposed by a psychic. Five years later, the sheriff in charge of that case, along with a couple of other residents, were killed by a rabid dog. In late 1999, the press dubbed another local serial killer the Tooth Fairy. He was caught by police after kidnapping his intended third victim.

In the early 1990s, Stephen decided it was time to close the book on Castle Rock, setting the downtown on fire. But Castle Rock bounced back. During the late 1990s, the town was still holding its Summerfest, the Castle County Crafts Co-op was in full swing, there were fireworks over the lake, and the hospital (St. Stephen's) was in operation. The town has a Gore-Tex factory and a Walmart. They even have a speedway (Castle Rock Speedway, of course). The annual Turkey Trot 12K race, which benefits the Castle View Recreational Park, brings in nearly a thousand runners from across New England, with the winner getting to light the Christmas tree in the Town Commons.

Sounds like a nice little town, doesn't it?

CHAPTER 3

Midas Touch
(1980s)

Stephen King's books appeared on a few bestseller lists during his first several years as a published novelist. However, it wasn't until the 1980s that he became a guaranteed bestseller. Every novel he published from that point forward debuted on the major bestseller lists during the book's first week of publication, often in the #1 position. Also, during the 1980s, hardly a year went by without at least one new feature film based on one of his novels or short stories being released. Everything Stephen touched turned to gold . . . but at what personal cost?

FIRESTARTER (1980)

After Stephen finished *The Dead Zone*, the family moved to England, where they planned to stay for a year. Stephen hoped to absorb enough of the country's landscape to write a book that would be set there. However, the only story inspired by the trip was "Crouch End," which he wrote after getting lost on the way to visit Peter Straub's home in the London neighborhood of the same name. During that visit, the two authors agreed to collaborate on a novel.

Drew Barrymore as Charlie McGee in the 1984 adaptation of *Firestarter*.

The Kings didn't make it through a full year, either. A number of reasons, including the constant cold they felt in their house, caused them to head back to Maine after only three months.

Firestarter arose from research Stephen had been doing into psychic phenomena, including reports of people inexplicably catching fire. He wanted to explore what might happen to someone who could control the ability to start fires with his or her mind. He also wanted to write about the uncontrolled power held by certain government agencies.

Stephen patterned his Firestarter, Charlie McGee, on his daughter, Naomi. "I know how she looks, I know how she walks, I know what makes her mad. . . . So I took Naomi, used her as the frame, and then went where I wanted."[53]

Stephen finished the final draft in the fall of 1978, writing at night while teaching creative writing at the University of Maine. The novel was published in September 1980 with a first printing of 100,000 copies. He was afraid the reviews were going to be terrible, but in general they were very positive. These translated into sales: Nearly 300,000 hardcover copies in the first year, a pretty big increase compared to *The Dead Zone*. This was also the first Stephen King book to be published in limited edition for collectors.

CUJO (1981)

Stephen completed *Cujo* during the family's stay in England, inspired by an encounter he'd had in the spring of 1977. His motorcycle wasn't running properly, so he took it to a mechanic who lived on a farm out in the middle of the countryside. Stephen barely made it to the farm before the cycle died on him. "The biggest Saint Bernard I ever saw in my life came out of that garage. . . . He started growling

RIGHT: King with a dog named *Cujo* at a book signing in Truth or Consequences, New Mexico, 1982. OPPOSITE: Handwritten manuscript page of the first draft of *Cujo*.

She took an involuntary step toward him and then stopped. She didn't believe those wives' tales about what might happen if you woke a sleepwalker — that the soul would be forever shut out of the body, or that madness would result, or death — and she hadn't needed Dr. Gresham to reassure her on that score. She had gotten a book on special loan from the Portland City Library. But she hadn't really needed that, either. Her own good common sense had told her that what happened when you woke a sleepwalker was that they woke up — no more nor less than that. There might be tears, even mild hysteria, but that sort of reaction would be provoked by simple disorientation.

But she had never wakened Brett during one of his nightwalks and she didn't dare to do so now. Good common sense was one thing. Her unreasoning fear was another — and this morning she was suddenly very afraid, and unable to say why. What could be so dreadful in Brett's acted-out dream of feeding his dog? It was perfectly natural, as worried as he had been about Cujo —

He was bent over now, holding the gravy boat out, the drawstring of his pajama trousers making a right-angled white line to the horizontal plane of the red-and-black linoleum floor. His face went through a slow-motion pantomiming of sorrow. He spoke then, muttering the words the way sleepers do, gutterally, rapidly, almost unintelligibly... and with no emotion; that was all inside, held in the cocoon of whatever dream had been vivid enough to make him nightwalk again, after all these years. There was nothing inherently melodramatic about the words, spoken all of a rush in a quick, sleeping sigh, but her hand went to her throat anyway, and the flesh there was cold, cold.

"Cujo's not hungry no more," Brett sighed. He stood up again, now holding the gravy boat cradled to his chest. "Cujo's not hungry no more, not no more."

He stood immobile for a short time by the counter, and Charity did likewise by the kitchen door. A single tear had slipped down his face. He put the gravy boat on the counter then and headed for the door. His eyes were open but they at me, way down in his throat. . . . At that time I weighed about 220 pounds, so I outweighed the dog by maybe ten pounds." The mechanic assured Stephen the dog didn't bite, so he reached out to pet the dog and it went for him. The man walked over to the dog and gave him a whack with a socket wrench. The dog yelped and sat down. "Bowser usually doesn't do this," the man said. "He must not have liked your face."[54]

Stephen still owned the Ford Pinto he had purchased with his advance from *Carrie*. He wanted to see if he could set a novel almost entirely in that car. Originally, Stephen thought the central conflict of *Cujo* would arise from Donna Trenton contracting rabies. The book would focus on her struggle to keep from hurting her son as she was overwhelmed by madness. "As I started to read about rabies, I found out that it takes

LEFT: A rabid Cujo stares down Donna and Tad Trenton in their Ford Pinto in the film adaptation of *Cujo*. BELOW: Stephen King in his home office.

GRAPHIC NOVELS

Graphic novel/comic book adaptations of Stephen's stories have been around since early in his career. In 1981, his short story "The Lawnmower Man" was adapted in Marvel's *Bizarre Adventures* #29. The next year, Bernie Wrightson created a comic-book adaptation of the five stories from the movie *Creepshow*.

Between 2007 and 2017, Marvel adapted the *Dark Tower* series, releasing approximately eighty-five issues that expanded upon parts of the first four books. *The Stand* also received the graphic novel treatment from Marvel between 2008 and 2012, with the unabridged story told in thirty-one issues. There have been similar adaptations of *The Talisman* and *Sleeping Beauties*, as well as graphic novels based on several of his short stories.

a lot longer to develop than I'd thought. Then the game became: 'Let's see if we can put them in one place in such a way that nobody will find them for the length of time that it takes for them to work out their problem, or for their problem to work them out.' Because it's always one way or another. When we're faced with a problem, either we solve it or it solves us."[55]

Cujo was a standard novel with chapters when Stephen first wrote it, but he took out all the breaks while revising the manuscript. "I can remember thinking that I wanted the book to feel like a brick that was heaved through your window at you. . . . It should get in your face. It should upset you, disturb you."[56]

Stephen's most controversial decision was allowing Tad Trenton to die. It wasn't a conscious choice, he has said; it just happened. He knew readers wouldn't like this ending, and being a people pleaser, he tried to rewrite it so Tad would live, but it didn't feel true to the story. In later years, Stephen has said he does not remember rewriting much of *Cujo*, owing to his dependence on alcohol at the time.

THE DARK TOWER

The Gunslinger (1982), *The Drawing of the Three* (1987), *The Waste Lands* (1991), *Wizard and Glass* (1997), *Wolves of the Calla* (2003), *Song of Susannah* (2004), *The Dark Tower* (2004), *The Wind Through the Keyhole* (2012)

Stephen was only twenty-one years old when he wrote the famous opening line of the Dark Tower series: "The man in black fled across the desert, and the gunslinger followed." His inspirations included the poetry of Robert Browning, spaghetti Western movies starring Clint Eastwood, and *The Lord of the Rings*.

The Dark Tower series is considered by many to be Stephen's greatest achievement. However, based on audience surveys that he occasionally conducted during public appearances, Stephen concluded that half of his Constant Readers hadn't read the series.

The five stories that comprise *The Gunslinger*, the first book in the series, were originally published in *The Magazine of Fantasy and Science Fiction* between 1978 and 1981. They were then collected in a limited edition of 10,000 copies by a small publishing company in Rhode Island. The book escaped the notice of most casual Stephen King fans until it was listed with his other titles at the front of *Pet Sematary* in 1983.

Fans bombarded Stephen and his publisher with letters asking how to get their hands on a copy of the book. Stephen thought that the story would have limited appeal to his regular readers, but he underestimated the appetite for his work. He authorized a second printing, but that did little to meet the demand. Ultimately, Stephen allowed the book to be published in paperback in 1988, making it available to a wider audience. Later he would revise *The Gunslinger* to add references to things that happened toward the end of the series.

Three more books in the series appeared over the next decade, *The Drawing of the Three* in 1987, *The Waste Lands* in 1991, and *Wizard and Glass* in 1997. Some of Stephen's determination to continue the series came from the ongoing demand for new installments from readers.

Even when he wasn't writing Dark Tower novels, he was thinking about it. During the 1990s, ideas from the series began to make their way into his other novels. When Peter Straub suggested they add Dark Tower elements to their collaborative novel *Black House*, Stephen replied, "I don't know if I can keep it out. At this point, everything I write is connected to it."[57]

The Dark Tower series unifies much of Stephen's fiction. "I am coming to understand that Roland's world (or worlds) actually contains all the others of my making," he once said.[58] A prominent theme in his work is that reality is thin and there are countless, perhaps infinite, parallel universes adjacent to one another with only thin curtains separating them. Under certain conditions, people can pass through "thinnies" to find themselves in another universe. These parallel realities are bound together by the Dark Tower, which looks different in different universes. In the most important reality, it is a pink rose in a vacant lot.

The epic fantasy of the Dark Tower series, blended with the feel of a classic Western and elements of horror and science fiction, is ultimately a tale of good versus evil. Roland and his followers (his "ka-tet") represent the white, supported by a mysterious force known as "ka" that wants them to succeed. The opposing force, the red, is led by the Crimson King and his minions, including Randall Flagg from *The Stand*. Roland's goal is to preserve reality, while the Crimson King wants to topple the Dark Tower so he can rule the resulting chaos.

The series also explores the act of writing. Because the early novels weren't copyedited before publication, mistakes crept in. Stephen made mistakes about geography or changed the names and ages of characters between books. He decided to incorporate these errors into the books, suggesting they weren't mistakes but rather details from nearly parallel but slightly different realities. The person who made these mistakes is Stephen himself. The Crimson King wants to stop the fictional version of him from writing a successful ending to Roland's quest. Stephen uses events from his own life and career as part of the narrative.

The series explores deep questions of existence. Roland is a tool of the universe, but an imperfect one. He is strong and determined enough to fulfill his destiny, but sufficiently flawed that he fails at his personal goal—to understand the nature of reality. Stephen seems to say that Roland's excessive pride and confidence is his curse, and only when he can free himself of the desire to conquer the Tower will he truly succeed.

Usually, when Stephen finds a story difficult going, he abandons it. However, he kept going back to the story of the *Dark Tower* every five years or so, even though progress was difficult.

After Stephen's near-fatal accident in 1999, he decided to finish the series once and for all. Starting in 2001, Stephen worked on little else but the last three books for sixteen months straight, producing over 2,500 manuscript pages. The unrelenting pace and the notion of finishing a lifelong work took its toll, and in June 2002 he took a one-month break to recharge his batteries. He finished the seventh and final book in Bangor, where he had begun the series over thirty years earlier.

As he neared the end of the series, he told a reporter he was ready to retire. He later dismissed these plans as the words of someone exhausted from the epic writing journey he had just undergone. In fact, he has been every bit as prolific since finishing the series as he was before.

In the years since the publication of the seventh and "final" volume, the Dark Tower universe has continued to grow. There has been a film adaptation and a failed series pilot from Amazon, and Marvel expanded upon stories of Roland's youth in graphic novels. Director Mike Flanagan plans to adapt the Dark Tower as a series for a streaming platform.

Elements from the series have continued to appear in his work. In 2009, Stephen asked readers via his website which of two books they'd like to see him work on next: a sequel to *The Shining* or a new Dark Tower novel. With nearly 12,000 votes cast, the two titles ended in a dead heat, separated by fewer than fifty votes. Ultimately, Stephen decided to work on the Dark Tower novel *The Wind Through the Keyhole* first.

DANSE MACABRE (1981)

In November 1978, Stephen's former editor, Bill Thompson, asked if he would be interested in writing a book about horror in movies, television, and radio. The concept intrigued Stephen, but he wasn't enthusiastic about the project at first. However, Thompson was persuasive and Stephen saw the book as something he could use for a class he was going to teach the next semester called "Themes in Supernatural Literature."

Stephen and Thompson decided to limit what the book covered to the previous thirty years or so, ending in 1980. He chose the 1950s as his starting point because there weren't many horror books or movies in the 1940s. Also, the 1950s represented the beginning of his personal experience with the genre. Stephen said later that he found it a very difficult book to write. It involved a lot of research, but he didn't want it to look that way in the final product.

DIFFERENT SEASONS (1982)
Rita Hayworth and Shawshank Redemption, Apt Pupil, The Body, The Breathing Method

Sometimes, when Stephen is working on a book, he gets an idea for another story. He can't stop working on the novel in progress, so he got in the habit of telling the stories to himself while he was going to sleep at night instead of counting sheep. He often has several of these "bedtime stories" going on at the same time and many are never written down.

But some are. "I had these three stories. . . . I sent them to Alan Williams, who was then my editor, and I said, 'What would you think about doing these things as a book? It's different, but the stories are pretty good.' And he said, 'Well, if there was another one, we could call it *Seasons*, and it would be great if there was one season that was similar to what you do.' I thought, Oh, then I could call the book *Different Seasons*, and people would get the idea that it was a little bit different."[59] Stephen says the four stories were "written for love, not money."[60] Each was written in a different house—three in Maine and one in Colorado, and only one of them is supernatural.

The Body, often seen as one of Stephen's most autobiographical stories, was actually inspired by an anecdote told to him by his college roommate, George McCloud, to whom the novella is dedicated. McCloud and a gang of boys had gone to see the body of a dog someone found next to the train tracks. Stephen didn't think people would be interested in a dead dog, so he turned it into a boy. The incident with the leeches did happen to Stephen—he and his friends went into a pond near the house where he grew up and came out covered with them.

With the book's publication, there were some who wondered if Stephen had reached the end of his fascination with "ghouls, ghosts, vampires, and unspeakable things lurking in the closets of little kids."[61] His editor was equally worried Stephen might be drifting away from the supernatural, so Stephen told him about his idea for the next novel: a haunted car.

TYPECAST WRITER

Stephen has such a reputation as a horror writer that people sometimes refuse to believe certain movies adapted from his works have anything to do with him. The producers of *Stand by Me*, based on his novella *The Body* from *Different Seasons*, did not use his name to promote the film because they didn't want audiences to think it was a horror movie.

Two other well-known movies, *The Green Mile* and *The Shawshank Redemption*, are also not widely recognized as adaptations of Stephen's work. However, it's one thing for people to debate this among themselves and another for someone to argue the point with the author himself, which is exactly what happened when Stephen was in a grocery store in Florida.

He later recounted the scenario to an interviewer, "This woman comes up to me and she goes, 'I know who you are! You're that horror writer. You're Stephen King.' I said, 'Yes, guilty as charged.' She said, 'I don't read what you do. I respect what you do, but I don't read it. Why don't you do something uplifting sometime, like that *Shawshank Redemption*?' I said, 'I did write that.' She said, 'No, you didn't.' It was surreal. . . . It was weird."[62]

CHRISTINE (1983)

The roaring engine that became *Christine* rolled off the assembly line as a short story idea inspired by the old, decrepit red Cadillac that Stephen owned in 1978. "One night as I was turning into my driveway, I saw the odometer numbers on my car turn from 9999.9 to 10,000. I found myself wondering if there might not be a story in an odometer that ran backward." He decided to use a 1958 Plymouth Fury because he didn't want to use a vehicle with a legend already attached to it. He thought the car (and perhaps the kid who owned it) would get younger. "The kicker would be that, when the odometer returned to zero, the car, at the height of its beauty, would spontaneously fall into component parts."[63] As he worked on the book, he became more interested in the interaction between Arnie Cunningham and Dennis Guilder. He also wanted to explore the relationship between these teenagers and their parents.

In addition to being about a haunted car, the novel is fueled by the rock-and-roll music Stephen has listened to all his life. He paid roughly $15,000 to obtain permission to use song lyrics at the beginning of each chapter, something he added after finishing the first draft. He was often quoted $50 for the use of a song per thousand copies printed. It didn't sound like much until he realized there were going to be 300,000 hardcover copies and even more paperbacks.

Stephen considers *Christine* his first true horror novel since *The Shining* because it offers no rational explanation for supernatural events. He surprised himself with how dark the story turned out. "I didn't like it very much because the whole thing started out to be sort of a joke. It was like *Happy Days* gone mad: boy gets car, boy loses car, boy finds car. I thought it was hilarious until the kid started to run people down. Because some stories get out of control and they are like the car itself: They start to run by themselves and they don't always turn out the way you think they are going to turn out."[64]

A technical problem facing Stephen arose from the fact that Dennis, the first-person narrator, is injured and spends weeks in the hospital, meaning he had to write the middle section of the book in the third person. He recalls speaking with Alan D. Williams, his editor at Viking, about his insecurities about the book. The two men were canoeing on the lake at Stephen's summer house. "I told Alan that I didn't like the way the book had turned out and said I was afraid no one would like it. . . . I thought the combination [of first and third person] ugly and awkward. I suggested we think about not publishing the book." Williams saw *Christine* as a love story. "The kids will get it," he reassured Stephen.[65]

For years, Stephen cited *Christine* as one of his worst-reviewed novels, and he's not sure why. He's said that he doesn't really think there is anything wrong with the book, even though the critics do.

CYCLE OF THE WEREWOLF (1983)

Stephen agreed to the project that became *Cycle of the Werewolf* when a young publisher named Christopher Zavisa approached him at the World Fantasy Convention in 1979. Zavisa wanted to make a calendar and asked Stephen to come up with twelve related vignettes, each to be accompanied by a painting and a calendar grid. The monthly concept made Stephen think of the phases of the moon, which drew him to thoughts of werewolves. He decided to stage a full moon during whatever holiday took place in each month. He apologizes in the book's afterword for taking "a good many liberties with the lunar cycle," calling it creative license.

The limitation of 500 words per installment worried Stephen more than anything else, because he felt it stifled his creativity. Intending to finish the project in less than two weeks, he wrote the first three installments and then set it aside for four months. Stephen wrote the April, May, and June sections while on vacation; however, he wasn't happy with the project until the story of Marty Coslaw and the murder that canceled the Fourth of July fireworks came to him. It went well beyond 500 words, but he didn't care. When he was finished up to September, Stephen broke the news to Zavisa— this couldn't be a calendar, but it could be a slim book. As it turns out, Zavisa wasn't disappointed. In fact, Stephen suspects a book might have been what the publisher was after all along, but he didn't have the courage to ask for one.

PET SEMATARY (1983)

In 1978, Stephen was invited to be writer-in-residence at the English department of his alma mater, the University of Maine, located in Orono, a few miles from Bangor. Stephen agreed, partly to thank the university for its support of him as a young writer. Among the classes he taught were Introduction to Creative Writing and a course on the literature of the fantastic, the notes from which he would use for *Danse Macabre*.

A pet in a cemetery: King and one of nearly twenty cats who played the General in the movie *Cat's Eye*. INSET: The sign for a "PETS SEMATARY" at a burial ground not far from the house King and his family rented during his tenure at the University of Maine.

During his time at the university, Stephen and his family moved into a rented house on a major highway in Orrington. The heavy traffic included trucks heading to and from a nearby chemical plant. A new neighbor warned the Kings to keep their pets away from the road, which, the neighbor said, had "used up a lot of animals."[66] In support of this claim, the Kings discovered a burial ground not far from the house, with "PETS SEMATARY" written on a sign in a child's handwriting. Among its residents: dogs, cats, birds, and a goat.

Shortly after they moved in, Stephen's daughter Naomi's cat Smucky was found dead on the side of the road when they returned from a trip to town. Stephen's first impulse was to tell Naomi the cat had wandered away. Tabby, however, believed this was a teachable moment. They broke the news to their daughter and conducted a feline funeral, committing Smucky's remains to the pet cemetery. A few nights later, Stephen discovered Naomi in the garage, jumping up and down on sheets of bubble wrap, indignant over the loss of her pet. "He was my cat. Let God have his own cat," she was repeating.[67]

The road almost "used up" the Kings' youngest son, too. Owen was about eighteen months old when he wandered dangerously close to the highway. To this day, Stephen isn't sure whether he knocked his son down before he reached the highway as one of the tankers approached or whether Owen tripped over his own feet. This near miss was an unwelcome reminder of the fragility of their children.

Even someone who isn't a writer would obsess over the possible outcomes of that incident, the "what ifs" that drive the creative impulse. Stephen felt compelled to explore the aftermath of a grimmer outcome, working in a room in the store across the street from their house. Naomi's reaction to the death of her cat and Owen's misadventure both made it into the book.

In the middle of 1979, six weeks after he finished writing *Pet Sematary*, Stephen reread the novel and decided it was too gruesome and disturbing to be published. Tabitha found the scene where two-year-old Gage Creed dies hard to deal with. Taking her advice, and that of his friend and fellow novelist Peter Straub, Stephen put the manuscript in a drawer. He intended for it to stay there forever, and he moved on to *The Dead Zone*. However, he mentioned the book in passing in response to an interview question about whether he had ever written anything too terrible to be published. A myth arose around the novel.

Pet Sematary would have remained in the drawer if not for an ongoing struggle with Doubleday. The contract he had signed with his original publisher contained a clause that allowed them to pay out his royalties at a rate of only $50,000 per year, while investing the rest. This practice allowed authors to defer taxes on this money. No one—including Stephen—could have anticipated how quickly his investment account would grow. By the early 1980s, Doubleday had millions of his dollars in reserve, and it would have taken the rest of his life for it to be paid out at the specified rate.

They reached an agreement to cancel the clause in the contract. If Stephen allowed them to publish another novel, Doubleday would release his accrued royalty money. However, the only manuscript available was *Pet Sematary*. After making sure Tabitha didn't object, Stephen agreed to give them the book. Because of his strong feelings about it, though, he refused to help the publisher promote it and rarely talked about it in interviews. Stephen said, "It's such a dreadful book, because you're welcomed into this family. It's a domestic drama. . . . The reason you grow to love them is that I loved them. And then it all falls down. And people say, 'Well, how could you do that?'"[68]

In the book, physician Louis Creed has just moved with his wife, Rachel, and two young children, Ellie and Gage, to the University of Maine. The family moves into a house in Ludlow very much like the one the Kings occupied in Orrington, with a busy highway out front and a pet cemetery nearby.

Louis thinks death is "except perhaps for childbirth, the most natural thing in the world." It isn't abstract. "We're all close, all the time," he tells his wife. As a doctor, he sees himself as somewhat above the laws of nature, though, because it is occasionally within his power to prevent death. However, he doesn't believe in an afterlife. "He had been present at many deathbeds and had never felt a soul bullet pass him on its way to . . . wherever." This includes the soul of Victor Pascow, the student struck by a car on Louis's first day of work, who delivered an ominous warning about the pet cemetery moments before he died.

The nearby animal burial ground prompts a discussion of death with Ellie, who is upset when she realizes her cat, Church, might die someday. Rachel doesn't want to talk about it. Her sister suffered horribly with spinal meningitis, and Rachel was alone with her on the day she died. The incident scarred her, and Louis learned early in their marriage to tread carefully around the topic of death. When Rachel and the

STEPHEN KING

The Eyes of the Dragon

Church the cat returns to life in this scene from the 1989 movie adaptation of *Pet Sematary*.

kids are visiting her parents, Church is hit by a truck and killed. Louis plans to bury his daughter's pet and pretend Church has simply wandered off. He's sparing Ellie's feelings, but he's also avoiding Rachel's refusal to deal with death.

Because Louis saved his elderly neighbor's wife, Jud Crandall repays the debt by leading Louis to a forsaken burial ground beyond the pet cemetery, an area legend says has been invaded by a mythical creature known as a Wendigo. Jud buried his own dog there when he was ten.

Church comes back the next afternoon, looking much the same as before but now smelling of dirt and death, no matter how many times he's washed. He doesn't purr anymore, either. Even though Jud knows the animals that come back from the burial ground are fundamentally changed, he feels this is a lesson for children—they need to know that sometimes dead is better.

Pet Sematary also explores the topic of burial practices and customs, making it a dark novel, but it becomes very bleak indeed when Stephen recreates the incident that inspired the book. However, rather than giving readers details about Gage's death, Stephen begins the book's second section with Louis talking about his son's funeral. Stephen foreshadowed that something sinister is about to happen at the end of the previous section by discussing the last happy day of Louis's life.

Naturally, Gage's death devastates the family. Louis is so blindsided his mind turns to the unthinkable. If Church came back, then so can Gage. After taking his readers through the grim events of Gage's visitation, including a struggle between Louis and his father-in-law that nearly knocks over Gage's coffin, Louis pretends none of this happened. However, his dream that everything is all right is the only moment in the final third of the novel with any hint of optimism. It's the writer's "what if" cast in a different direction.

What follows is one of the most discomforting and harrowing passages in all of Stephen's fiction. Louis sends Rachel and Ellie to Chicago to stay with Rachel's parents while he puts his misguided plan into effect. Intellectually, he accepts that he might have to kill Gage if his son comes back altered. However, he's also planning the family's escape to a new location if Gage comes back normal. They wouldn't be able to stay in Ludlow with a resurrected son, after all.

The final element in this family tragedy is initiated by Ellie. She dreams about Gage's coffin being empty and about the student who died on Louis's first day at work. When Rachel hears this, she returns alone to Maine. Stephen says Rachel made that decision on her own: "I didn't make her come back, I didn't say she would come back. She just ran back. Because characters get away sometimes and they start to go on their own and all you can do is hope that they go in a place that won't make the book too uncomfortable for you."[69]

The police almost catch Louis in the act of digging up his son's body. In a gruesome touch of realism, Louis thinks his son's head is missing only to discover moss has grown on the corpse after his burial.

Gage returns as a homicidal monster. His first victim is Jud Crandall. Next comes Gage's mother, who shows up at the most inconvenient moment. Rachel's death drives Louis beyond the brink of sanity. Rationalization kicks in—he lists all the reasons why things went wrong with Gage and how things might work better for his newly deceased wife. Louis hasn't learned his lesson. He makes one last trip to the burial ground and then waits for Rachel to return.

The last line of the novel is one of the most devastating in Stephen's works. Rachel's hand is cold and her voice is gravelly as she says, "Darling." The speaker of this word is identified as "it" rather than "she."

What happens next is left as an exercise for the reader.

THE EYES OF THE DRAGON (1984)

By the age of thirteen, Stephen's daughter, Naomi, was an avid reader, but she hadn't read any of her father's books. Her mother pushed her to read some horror, thinking it would be another way for her to know her father. However, Naomi made it clear she had "very little interest in [his] vampires, ghoulies and slushy crawling things." He asked her what she did like, and she told him she liked dragons. "I decided that if the mountain would not go to Mohammed, then Mohammed must go to the mountain."[70]

Stephen started working on the story, originally called *The Napkins*, in their house in western Maine, not intending for the book to be published. He wrote on a yellow legal pad in front of a woodstove while a wild storm blew snow across the frozen lake outside. Stephen had recently been working on *The Talisman*, so the fantasy land of the Territories was fresh in his mind. He wrote *The Eyes of the Dragon* at the same time as he was writing *Misery*, working on one book in the morning and the other at night. He completed the first draft in 1983.

Naomi, Stephen admits, was less than enthusiastic about the manuscript, but he was rewarded. The story kidnapped her and the only thing wrong with it, she told him later, was that she didn't want it to end. Stephen says, "I did her the courtesy of writing *Eyes of the Dragon* for myself too, because if you are writing just for someone else, you always write down."[71] The book is dedicated to her and to Peter Straub's son, Ben, and characters bearing their names appear in the novel.

Stephen says that, like any children's story, it is also a story for grown-ups. He calls it an adult novel masquerading as a children's story. He decided to self-publish the book using Philtrum Press. Three years later, Stephen agreed to allow publication of a trade edition. Numerous changes were made to the text, which hadn't previously been copyedited.

OPPOSITE: Doubleday hardcover edition of *Pet Sematary*.

STEPHEN KING

A NOVEL
BY THE AUTHOR OF
THE SHINING AND CHRISTINE

PET SEMATARY

UNSEEN KING

A lot of Stephen King fans want to have everything he has published in all editions. The buying and selling of his limited editions is a cottage industry, and signed copies of his novels fetch high prices at online auction sites. Fake autographs have flooded the market, with people looking to take advantage of fans' desire to own something Stephen has signed.

Most of the signed limited editions of his books contain the same material as the trade editions. Although the production quality of these limited editions is higher, and most are illustrated, the text itself is identical to what's available in a paperback copy at a fraction of the price.

This isn't always the case, though, and only the most avid and determined fans will have copies of some of the rarer books and stories that have been produced throughout his career. Here are a few examples:

Firestarter: The first ever Stephen King limited edition consisted of a 725-copy numbered edition from Phantasia Press with a wraparound cover, and a twenty-six-copy lettered edition bound in asbestos, which remains one of the most sought-after and valuable Stephen King limited editions.

The Eyes of the Dragon: Stephen produced an oversized limited edition of this novel through Philtrum Press. Of the 1,250 copies printed, 250 were sent to friends at Christmas and the other 1,000 were offered to the public. This lavish edition is noteworthy because the text of the novel is significantly different from the trade edition.

Skeleton Crew: The limited edition from Scream Press is a visually stunning edition, with striking photo-realistic illustrations. The book is hefty, contains a fold-out poster, and has Stephen's signature in silver ink on black paper. It also contains an extra story not found in the Viking edition.

The Regulators: The lettered edition of this Richard Bachman novel is "signed" by Bachman in the form of canceled checks made out to various characters or businesses from Stephen's work.

Charlie the Choo-Choo: This book was originally produced for San Diego Comic-Con to promote the forthcoming movie *The Dark Tower.* An actress portraying Beryl Evans, the book's supposed author, signed copies at the convention. The text itself comes from the *Dark Tower* series.

THE TALISMAN (1984) AND BLACK HOUSE (2001) WITH PETER STRAUB

Stephen first encountered Peter Straub's work when he was sent a prepublication copy of *Julia* by Peter's publisher. Stephen wrote a blurb for the book's dust jacket that struck Straub as being particularly insightful. When Stephen and Peter met for drinks at a hotel in London, Stephen suggested they collaborate on a novel. They continued these discussions over dinner at the Straubs' house. The main problem was that the two authors had other commitments that prevented them from working together for a few years.

They batted around ideas each time they saw each other and worked out more details when the Straubs visited Maine. The roots of *The Talisman* came from an idea Stephen had in college about a kid trying to find something to save his mother's life. While Stephen didn't think he was capable of handling the story in college, Straub responded to the idea when he heard it later. Stephen says Straub's modifications to the concept injected enough vitality into it to get them going.

In 1981, they outlined the first half of the book during an intense three-day meeting in Straub's office and wrote the first chapters in the spring of 1982 on Straub's computer. After that, each author would write for three or four weeks at a time until he reached a point where he was comfortable handing it off to the other. They sent the manuscript back and forth using a telephone modem between two completely different computer systems. To fool readers, each author occasionally imitated the other's style, and there were times during copyediting when Stephen wasn't sure who had written what.

By late November 1982, the book was growing very long, and they still hadn't mapped out the second half. The two families met in a hotel in Boston. After everyone else went to bed, Stephen and Straub radically streamlined the ending. They later worked on the final chapters together at Stephen's house. They'd only made it a quarter of the way through their original outline. If they'd stuck to the plan, *The Talisman* would have ended up 4,000 pages long.

In April 1999, Stephen and Straub got together again in Florida to create a long outline for a sequel to *The Talisman*. They were curious to discover what happened to Jack Sawyer in the decades since they first wrote about him. "For guys like us, finding things out means writing things down. Imagination can take guys like us anywhere, but you have to engage it first, and that means writing. We decided to engage."[72] Two months later, Stephen was involved in a major accident, which delayed their start on the project until February 2000.

Straub wrote the first fifty pages and sent them to Stephen as an email attachment. They continued exchanging increasingly longer sections without editing the other person's work. "It's like playing tennis, we drew the court, a synopsis, and now we just bat this thing back to each other on email," Stephen said.[73] "I enjoyed the process the second time even more than the first because it seemed to me to actually be a richer book in some ways . . . it's the same for writers as it is for readers when you go back and revisit characters that you've written about before, they become real in your imagination and it's like meeting old friends."[74]

Since Stephen was still recovering from his accident, he did not participate in most interviews leading up to the book's release. He was scheduled to be on a morning talk show with Peter in New York the week it came out. However, *Black House* was published by Random House on September 13, 2001, two days after the terrorist attacks on America. Stephen called Peter and said he wasn't sure that after what had just happened anyone was going to want to read a book about a series of murders.

The book's ending seems to imply the two authors could continue the story with a third novel. However, Peter died in 2022. King has since said he might write the third book himself using notes Peter sent him for inspiration.

SKELETON CREW (1985)

The Mist, "Here There Be Tygers," "The Monkey," "Cain Rose Up," "Mrs. Todd's Shortcut," "The Jaunt," "The Wedding Gig," "Paranoid: A Chant," "The Raft," "Word Processor of the Gods," "The Man Who Would Not Shake Hands," "Beachworld," "The Reaper's Image," "Nona," "For Owen," "Survivor Type," "Uncle Otto's Truck," "Morning Deliveries (Milkman #1)," "Big Wheels: A Tale of the Laundry Game (Milkman #2)," "Gramma," *The Ballad of the Flexible Bullet*, "The Reach"

Even as Stephen's book-writing career was taking off, he continued to publish short stories at an impressive pace in the 1980s. According to the inaugural issue of the *Castle Rock* newsletter (published by Stephen's sister-in-law and office manager, Stephanie Leonard), Stephen's second collection was originally to be called *Night Moves*. Ultimately renamed *Skeleton Crew*, it collected twenty-two stories and poems, some of which had been rejected by Bill Thompson for *Night Shift*. Three stories from the book were originally published in the late 1960s, one in the 1970s, and the remaining stories were published for the first time in the 1980s.

THINNER (1984)

In the early 1980s, Stephen weighed 236 pounds and was smoking heavily. His doctor told him, "In case you haven't noticed it, you've entered heart attack country."[75] After a weekend spent reacting negatively to the doctor's advice that he quit smoking and lose weight, Stephen decided to comply. "Once the weight actually started to come off, I began to realize that I was attached to it somehow, that I didn't really want to lose it. I began to think about what would happen if somebody started to lose weight and couldn't stop."[76]

From this experience sprang the beginnings of a short story called "Gypsy Pie," which blossomed into a novel, written in 1982–3 immediately after he finished *Misery*. "*Thinner* is a story about responsibilities. It's about coming to grips with your responsibilities and what happens when you don't. If you avoid your obligations, then you always end up hurting your loved ones," he said.[77]

However, Stephen had a problem: He had two books in the publication pipeline and three other manuscripts finished, with more in progress. Publishers used to believe the market could only handle one new book from a major author per year. Stephen had already challenged that by averaging two per year for several years, but even at that pace, *Thinner* wouldn't see print for several years.

Stephen decided to resurrect his old pseudonym, Richard Bachman. He'd thought he'd gone as far as he could with that pen name, but he was still curious as to whether he could break Bachman out. Had Stephen's success been a fluke? He said, "It is for some reason depressing to think it was all—or even mostly—an accident. So maybe you try to find out if you could do it again."

New American Library produced a special edition of the novel—Bachman's first hardcover original—for booksellers that contained a letter praising the book's merits. To help sustain the illusion, Stephen's agent supplied a photograph of an old friend to use as the author photo on the dust jacket. The first four books published by Bachman had been early works, and none were supernatural horror, whereas this was recent and very much a horror novel. An early review said *Thinner* was "what Stephen King would write like if Stephen King could really write."

Rumors about the real identity of the book's author spread. When bookseller Stephen P. Brown found the "smoking gun" proof of Stephen's name on *Rage*'s copyright form and sent it to Stephen in early 1985, Stephen called Brown to provide background for an article in the *Washington Post*.[78] However, the *Bangor Daily News*

Robert John Burke as Billy Halleck in the 1996 adaptation of *Thinner*.

informed Stephen they were going to publish a story with or without a statement from him, so Stephen agreed to confirm the pseudonym and they got the scoop.

Irked by the fact that his experiment had been short-circuited, Stephen declared Richard Bachman dead. His obituary ran in *Castle Rock*. "Richard Bachman, 40(?) of New Hampshire (pick a town, make one up?) died of exposure February 9th, 1985. Bachman, a writer, is survived by his wife, Claudia Inez, and a half-brother, John Swithen. Bachman was a merchant seaman for many years before settling down on a dairy farm to write." In later interviews, the cause of death was modified to cancer of the pseudonym.

Rather than reprint the dust jacket after the revelation, NAL affixed a narrow paper band to each copy proclaiming, "Stephen King writing as Richard Bachman." Before this, *Thinner* had sold a respectable 28,000 copies. After the announcement, the book sold nearly another 300,000 copies in four printings.

IT (1986)

While Stephen was working on *The Stand*, he had an experience that was the seed for another long novel he would write many years later. When the Kings lived in Boulder, their family vehicle was an AMC Matador, "an admirable car right up until the day when its transmission just fell out onto Pearl Street."[79] Two days after the car was towed to a dealership on the east end of the city, Stephen received word it was ready to be picked up.

Rather than call a cab, Stephen decided he needed the exercise and walked the three miles to the dealership, eventually ending up on a narrow unlit road at twilight. He recalls the moment vividly: "I was aware of how alone I was. About a quarter of a mile along this road was a wooden bridge, humped and oddly quaint, spanning a stream. I walked across it. I was wearing cowboy boots with rundown heels, and I was very aware of the sound they made on the boards; they sounded like a hollow clock."[80] "I thought of the story of Billy Goats Gruff, the troll who says, 'Who's that trip-trapping on my bridge?' and the whole story just bounced into my mind on a pogo-stick. Not the characters, but the split time-frame, the accelerated bounces that would end with a complete breakdown, which might result in a feeling of 'no time,' all the monsters that were one monster . . . the troll under the bridge, of course."[81]

While Stephen worked on other projects over the next two years, the image of the troll returned to him. He saw the bridge as a symbol for transition. The book that developed from these notions is *It*, which Stephen thought of at the time as the end of a phase—the last book he intended to write about supernatural monsters and kids in jeopardy. "The book is the summation of everything I have done and learned in my whole life to this point,"[82] he said. "Every monster that ever lived is in this book. This is it, this is the final exam."[83]

It tells the stories of seven friends, outsiders who make up the self-anointed Losers' Club. Stephen says he wrote about children for so many years because he had small children of his own.[84] He believes a person can't truly finish with his childhood until his offspring have finished with theirs: "You get a kind of perspective on what your own childhood meant, what you went through," he said in an interview.[85] "The idea is to come back and confront your childhood, in a sense relive it if you can, so that you can be whole."[86]

The book moves smoothly back and forth between two eras—the 1950s of Stephen's youth, and the 1980s, when he was reflecting on that time as an adult.

Tim Curry as Pennywise the clown, the most familiar form of the monster from *It*, in a still from the 1990 miniseries.

"When I started to work on *It* . . . I realized that I was writing about the way we use our imaginations at different points in our lives."[87] Stephen claims that children are better capable of withstanding the creature they call Pennywise. That's because their developing minds still believe that a monster can appear differently to everyone who sees it—werewolf, mummy, giant pterodactyl—feeding on the fears that haunt the child's mind. Pennywise knows adults have a disadvantage against him because they have lost much of their imagination and sense of wonder at the world. After the members of the Losers' Club injure the monster, it decides to let them go and deal with them during its next cycle of strength when they are adults.

The book also explores how childhood memories grow vague with time. By 1985, when the grown-up Losers reassemble in the fictional and unlovely city of Derry, they recall little from 1958. Only Mike Hanlon, who has remained in the city and has been keeping notes about those long-ago events, remembers anything.

The 1958 "childhood" version of Derry is modeled after Stratford, Connecticut, where Stephen lived for a time as a child before moving to Maine. That was where he discovered The Barrens—the forsaken place where the Losers play. Stephen's older

A group shot of King with his childhood friends, circa June 1960. King is in the back row, far right.

In the novel, *It*, several children supposedly drowned over the years in the standpipe. In reality, an 11-year-old boy died after falling from a railing of Bangor's Thomas Hill standpipe in 1940.

brother, Dave, showed him how to dam the stream, and a cop very much like Mr. Nell appeared after the brothers flooded the neighborhood. The Derry Public Library where Mike Hanlon works is based on the library Stephen frequented in Stratford, and the corridor separating the adult section from the children's section represents another kind of bridge, a symbol of the transition between childhood and adulthood.

The most familiar form of Pennywise—the evil clown—came to Stephen while he was walking in downtown Bangor after a heavy rainstorm. He wondered whether an entire city could be haunted. Harkening back to the story of the Billy Goats Gruff, he

ABOVE: Publicity photo of King used by Viking Press in conjunction with the release of *It*.
BELOW: King clowns around with a German edition of *It* (translated *Es*).

visualized Bangor as a metaphor for the bridge: "The water was going down the gutter and running down the sewers. As I looked at this one sewer as I was going by, the voice inside speaks up again and says, 'The troll lives there too, only when he's in the sewers he has a clown suit on.'"[88]

The murder of Adrian Mellon, the first killing to catch adult Mike Hanlon's attention, is based on a real incident in Bangor in 1984. The victim did not drown after being thrown off the bridge into the stream—he suffocated because of his asthma, which Stephen likens to being frightened to death. Stephen took notes on the police interrogation at the time and fictionalized the murder as part of the 1985 sequence of events.

Although Derry shares some features with Bangor and other events from Bangor's history make it into the novel, the two cities are geographically distinct in Stephen's universe. Characters are aware of both places.

Even though Pennywise comes back to Derry every generation to plunder the city of its children, the city thrives. The adults have turned a blind eye to the city's dark underbelly, allowing evil free rein by simply doing nothing.

The seven Losers discover evil can prevail, but good can conquer evil if they band together. On their own, they are vulnerable, both to the town's bullies and to Pennywise. When they present a united front, they can defeat both.

Granted, they are not completely alone—a turtle acts as a counterforce to Pennywise. It claims to have created the universe but now prefers to hide in its shell and allow things to happen without interfering. To Stephen the turtle represents the stability and sanity that exists in a world that can be confusing and overwhelming.

Revisions to *It* were done at the end of Stephen's long days on the set of *Maximum Overdrive*, which he wrote and directed.

During the seven years between the inspiration for *It* and when he finished the book, Stephen's addiction problems expanded to include drugs. For nearly two years after completing *It*, Stephen wasn't able to finish anything except for a few short stories. "That's why, when Peter [Straub] and I made our way through *The Talisman*, and I began work on *The Tommyknockers* and *The Napkins* [i.e., *The Eyes of the Dragon*], I was so knocked over to learn that there was indeed life after *It*."[89]

MISERY (1987)

Misery started out as a novella called *The Annie Wilkes Edition*, inspired by a dream Stephen had during a flight to England in the early 1980s. He dreamed about "a woman who held a writer prisoner and killed him, skinned him, fed the remains to her pig, and bound his novel in human skin."[90] When he woke up, he wrote this scene on a cocktail napkin so he wouldn't forget it.

Stephen was unable to sleep after arriving in England, and the story continued to haunt him. He asked the concierge at Brown's Hotel in London for a quiet place where he could write. The man led him to a staircase landing where there was a desk that had once belonged to Rudyard Kipling, author of *The Jungle Book*. That night, Stephen filled sixteen pages of a notebook in longhand. He remembers, "When I called it quits, I stopped in the lobby to thank the concierge again for letting me use Mr. Kipling's beautiful desk. 'I'm so glad you enjoyed it,' he replied. 'Kipling died there, actually. Of a stroke. While he was writing.' I went back upstairs to catch a few hours' sleep, thinking of how often we are given information we really could have done without."[91]

(continued on page 90)

WELCOME TO DERRY

Thirty miles from Bangor, Derry was established in the 1740s in what appears to have been the most geographically unsuitable place the settlers could find. The native Micmac people had shunned this swampy and overgrown valley formed by the slow-moving Kenduskeag Stream, choosing instead to settle on a high wooded ridge above it.

The original English settlers were formally known as the Derrie Company. The land granted them under a charter covered what is today Derry, most of Newport, and little slices of the surrounding towns. The Penobscot River, into which the Kenduskeag flows, was great for traders. Not so good for farmers or for those who built their homes too close to these bodies of water, which had a habit of overflowing their banks every few years.

From its earliest days, strange things occurred in the town. Sometime between June and October 1741, all 340 people living in Derry Township disappeared, leaving their homes abandoned—except for one that burned to the ground. Historians claim they were slaughtered by natives, but there is no evidence to support that theory.

Derry became a lumber town because timber could be floated downriver to the sea. Any experienced city planner would have frowned at the decision to locate the city's downtown in the Kenduskeag valley, which runs through the business district on a diagonal from southwest to northeast. But that's what happened, with the rest of the town swarming up the sides of the surrounding hills.

The city has always been bad, described by one person as a place where reality is a thin skim of ice over a deep lake of dark water. A place where it always feels like it's thirteen o'clock. Acts of violence were regular occurrences in what would become Maine's fourth-largest city. In 1876, four loggers were found torn apart in a cabin. Four people were lynched in 1877, including a Methodist lay preacher who drowned his children and shot his wife, staging the scene to make it look like she committed suicide. There was a mass murder at the Silver Dollar in 1905. An explosion in 1906 at the Kitchener Ironworks on Easter Sunday killed 102, including eighty-eight kids. A group of bank robbers known as the Bradley Gang were gunned down on Canal Street in October 1929, and a year later, a fire at the Black Spot (a "special" barracks at the old Derry Army Air Force Base), killed sixty people.

A man was thrown from a bridge into the canal in 1984. A rash of murders and disappearances involving children has happened nearly every twenty-seven to twenty-eight years throughout the city's history, including half a dozen killings in 1984–85. Two state police officers disappeared without a trace in July 1988 and a third, in charge of investigating the disappearance, committed suicide. A man murdered his wife and twin daughters in 1996, posing their bodies at the dining room table. An investigative journalist was killed in a hit-and-run accident in 2019, although some people suspect it wasn't an accident.

The overgrown tangle that is the Kenduskeag valley became known as The Barrens, a messy tract of land about a mile and a half wide by three miles long that makes Derry look like a town whose heart has been pierced by a narrow green dagger. One side of the valley is a modern shopping mall (built on the site of the defunct Kitchener Ironworks) and Old Cape, a low-income housing development built in 1946 where the drainage is so bad there are stories of toilets and sewer-pipes exploding. The town's sewer system was built during the Great Depression, with the main sewage pumping stations installed in The Barrens.

Frequent flooding has brought misfortune to Derry. The 1931 flood caused millions in damage. Decades later, a little boy named Georgie Denborough was lost in the flood that overwhelmed the downtown in fall 1957. In an attempt to protect the downtown (which the old-timers call Low Town) against floods, the city spent vast amounts of money to encase two miles of the Kenduskeag in a concrete canal.

On May 31, 1985, the worst storm in Maine's history knocked over the standpipe at Carter Lookout (the site of a number of drownings over the years), unleashing three-quarters of a million gallons of water that flowed down Upmile Hill to Kansas Street, killing scores of people (fatality estimates range from sixty to over 200). Most of downtown Derry collapsed into the canal, which leads to the Kenduskeag, then to the Penobscot, and, ultimately, the Atlantic Ocean. A National Weather Service forecaster said it looked like the town had been struck by "some weird species of pocket hurricane," one that was limited almost exclusively to Derry Township. Much of Derry was severely damaged or destroyed by the flood of 1985, but the city rebuilt once more—although it remains "a dark and dreary town with a violent history."[92]

STEPHEN KING TOUR OF BANGOR

Since many fans travel to Bangor to see Stephen's house and locations from his novels, the Greater Bangor Convention and Visitors Bureau promotes a private company that offers three-hour, themed bus tours throughout the year.

Among the twenty to thirty destinations seen on the tour are the Standpipe, the Paul Bunyan statue, Mount Hope Cemetery (used during the filming of *Pet Sematary*), and Bangor's version of The Barrens. Other stops include sites from Stephen's past, among them the laundry where he worked after college and some of his early residences, as well as places the Kings' generosity helped construct or expand, such as the community swimming pool, the baseball field at Mansfield Park, and the Bangor Public Library.

The highlight of the tour is Stephen's home, with its wrought-iron fence featuring bats, spiders, and other intricate design elements. Out of respect for the family's privacy, the bus doesn't stop at their house, and the tour operators have an agreement with the Kings to ensure they won't drive by it too often.

The iconic house (as well as the adjacent house) has been proposed as the location of a writers' retreat. It will also house the offices of the Stephen and Tabitha King Foundation and holds Stephen's archives, which were formerly at the University of Maine. These documents will be available by appointment only for researchers and scholars. The location will not be open to the public because the Kings don't want to turn it into a museum that would disturb other people who live in the neighborhood.

(*continued from page 85*)

Misery was also inspired by John Fowles' *The Collector* and the Evelyn Waugh short story "The Man Who Loved Dickens." After reading the latter, Stephen wondered what would happen if Dickens himself were held captive. "And then I started to wonder, 'Well, what would that crazy person want?' And the answer seemed fairly obvious to me: that crazy person would want more stories, only written her way. The writer would in essence become a secretary for lunacy. And then I thought, 'If I were put in that position, could I do that?' And the answer was, 'Yes. To stay alive, I probably could do that, and a great deal more.'"[93]

Stephen also plays with *One Thousand and One Nights*, in which Scheherazade forestalls her execution by telling the King exciting stories and promising even better ones the following nights. The novella turned into a novel when Paul Sheldon fought back from the fate Stephen had conceived for him in his dream. "His efforts to play Scheherazade and save his life gave me a chance to say some things about the redemptive power of writing that I had long felt but never articulated."[94]

When asked why he wrote *Misery*, he responded: "I wrote it for the reason I write anything: it occurred to me as a story I wanted to hear myself. . . . I do remember thinking that it would be a great pleasure to finally have another character like Randall Flagg in *The Stand*, who was utterly and completely gonzo. Willing to do anything, not only to her 'pet writer' or any 'dirty bird' who happens to get in her way, but to herself. Halfway through, as in *Pet Sematary*, I realized I was trying to express some of my own deepest fears: the sense of being trapped . . . and knowing I would never be able to get home."[95]

Some readers interpreted the book as a message for his more demanding fans, especially because of the book's cryptic dedication. "This is for Stephanie and Jim Leonard, who know why. Boy, do they." Stephanie Leonard, Stephen's sister-in-law, was also his personal assistant at the time and the editor of *Castle Rock*, the monthly newsletter distributed from Stephen's office to over 5,000 subscribers. Stephen agreed to the newsletter in the mid-1980s in response to the flood of fan mail he was receiving. He answered frequently asked questions and even contributed works of fiction and nonfiction occasionally, as long as he wasn't directly involved with it. The publication was a family affair—Stephen's mother-in-law, Sarah Jane Spruce, also handled the subscriptions.

OPPOSITE: The Viking hardcover edition of *Misery*.

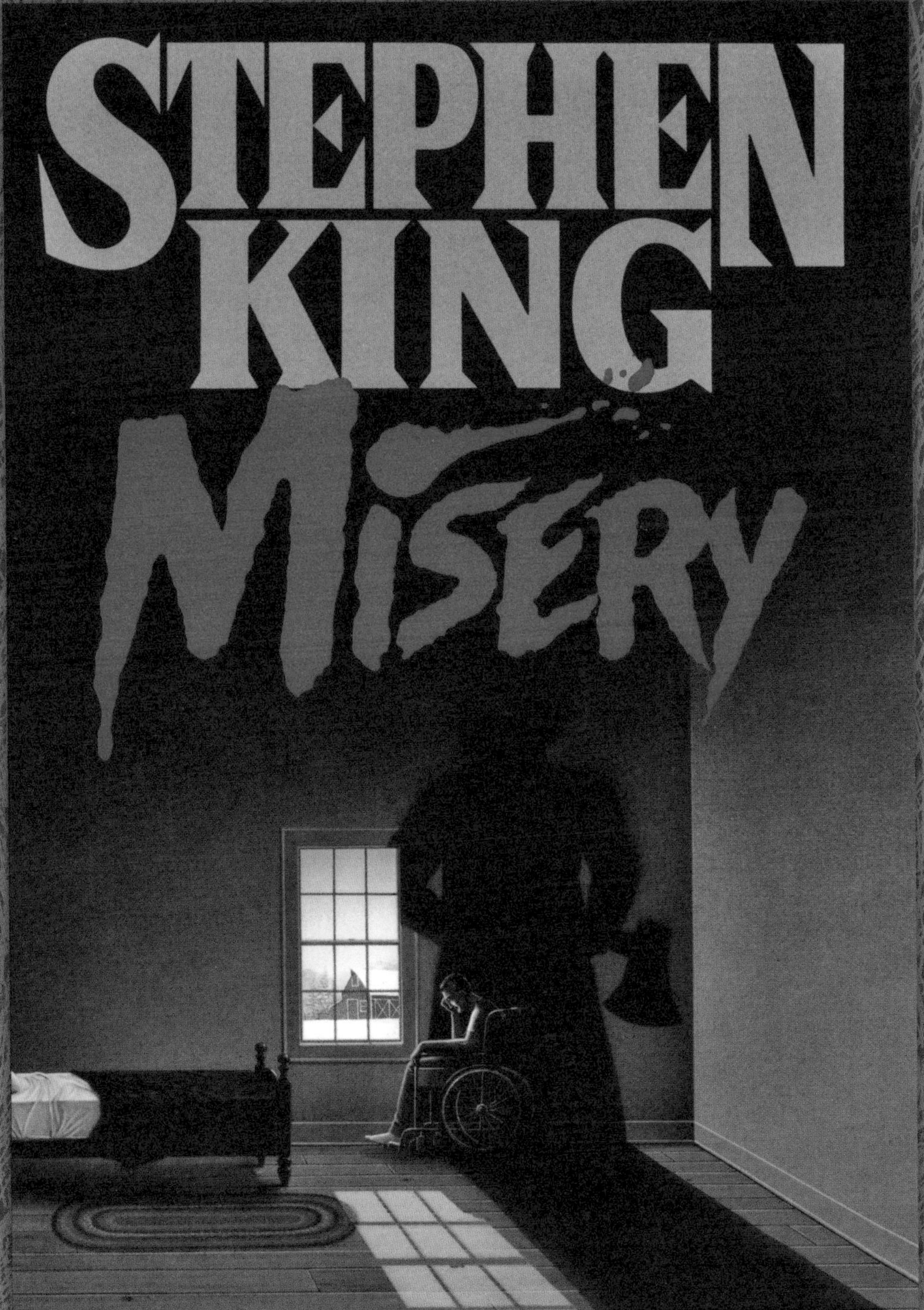
STEPHEN
KING
MISERY

Although Stephen sees *Misery* as a love letter to his fans, the fans weren't so sure. Tabitha King responded to their letters with an essay in *Castle Rock* that said in part, "I have read several pained, angry, and offended letters from fans who mistakenly believe that Steve was recording his true feelings about his readers in *Misery*. I take their distress as genuine and want to ease it if I can. If [Annie Wilkes] personifies any fan, it is perhaps Mark Chapman. [Mark Chapman is an obsessive Beatles fan who fatally shot John Lennon on December 8, 1980.] Celebrity attracts madness as well as whole people. . . . Perhaps more importantly, Annie Wilkes is a metaphor for the creative drive itself. . . . *Misery* is concerned with the way in which a creative person can be tortured by his own powers, addicted to the act of creation, damaged by it."[96]

In the book, Stephen's overzealous fan, Annie Wilkes, is given unique access to the object of her obsession, Paul Sheldon, the author of Victorian romance novels featuring heroine Misery Chastain. Annie is a former nurse once charged with killing patients in her neonatal ward. She was acquitted, but she was guilty of those and numerous other killings during her career.

Paul appears like a gift when he veers off the road during a snowstorm. He has just celebrated the completion of his first mainstream novel. For years he has felt pigeonholed as a romance writer, and he believes *Fast Cars* might win both critical acclaim and prestigious literary awards. The only copy of the manuscript in existence, the result of two years' work, is with him when he crashes.

Annie stumbles upon the scene and rescues him from the wreckage. Both of Paul's legs are broken and he is unconscious, but instead of taking him to the hospital, Annie brings him to her isolated house, where she intends to nurse her idol back to health. Paul awakens to find himself immobilized in bed and heavily medicated.

Annie discovers and reads *Fast Cars*. She doesn't like it, and forces Paul to burn the manuscript. Paul is still in incredible pain from the accident, and she threatens to withhold his medication to coerce him into complying.

Annie can't afford to buy Paul's books in hardcover, so she doesn't know yet that Paul killed off the heroine in his latest book, *Misery's Child*. Once she finds out, she is enraged—but she also has a solution at her disposal: the creator is under her complete control. She acquires all the things Paul needs to set up an office and tells him to write a novel that resurrects Misery from the dead. The only way Paul can prolong his life and perhaps find a way to escape is to tell Annie the story she wants to hear, the next Misery Chastain novel. Properly motivated, he pours his heart and soul into the book and is surprised to discover that it's the best one he's ever written.

After Annie amputates Paul's foot with an axe following one of his escape attempts, and cauterizes the stump with a propane torch, there's no longer any question about her sanity. At first, Stephen thought that Annie should have a good side, because everyone does—or so he believed. But he says that, ultimately, "this voice rose up inside me and said, 'Why does she have to have a good side? If she's crazy, go ahead, make her a monster! She's a human being but let her be a monster if that's what she wants to be,' and it was such a relief!"[97]

One of the amusing details in the book is the old Royal typewriter Annie buys for Paul that is missing the letter *N*, like the one Stephen used as a child to write his first stories. Like Stephen, Paul enters the missing letters by hand, an effect that is recreated in the extracts of Paul's manuscript.

In a real-life twist that might have come from one of his books, a woman sued Stephen over *Misery*, claiming Annie Wilkes was based on her. She also believed Stephen tapped her phone, hired helicopters to spy on her, burglarized her home, and stole manuscripts, which he later published under his name.

THE TOMMYKNOCKERS (1987)

The Tommyknockers had its origins in a short story idea King had when he was a senior in college, about a guy stumbling over a flying saucer. He wrote fifteen to twenty pages but stopped, because "the canvas was just too big"[98] and he didn't feel like he had enough understanding of the central character Jim Gardner's self-loathing at the time.

The pages were lost. "Years later the idea recurred and I just got swept up by the concept. I can remember going into that book thinking, if I have these two people and they're able to get this flying saucer out of the ground and fly it, then they can decide they're going to become sheriffs for world peace and discover they do a really terrible job at it, because power corrupts and absolute power corrupts absolutely. But it turned out not to be that."[99]

The title was drawn from a piece of childhood verse of unknown origin. The word refers to ghosts that haunt deserted mines or caves, perhaps the spirits of miners who died of starvation as they knocked on the timbers to be rescued.

A terrifying
descent into evil.

From the master
of horror!

STEPHEN KING'S
THE
TOMMYKNOCKERS

STEPHEN KING'S "THE TOMMYKNOCKERS" Starring JIMMY SMITS • MARG HELGENBERGER Music by CHRISTOPHER FRANKE Edited by TOD FEUERMAN
Production Designer BERNARD HIDES Director of Photography DANNY BURSTALL • DAVID EGGBY Co-Producer LAWRENCE D. COHEN Executive Producer FRANK KONIGSBERG • LARRY SANITSKY
Produced by JAYNE BIEBER • JANE SCOTT Teleplay by LAWRENCE D. COHEN Based on the novel by STEPHEN KING Directed by JOHN POWER

THE
KONIGSBERG SANITSKY
COMPANY

King said, "*The Tommyknockers* is . . . about our obsession with gadgets. . . . Our technology has outraced our morality. And I don't think it's possible to stick the devil back in the box."[100]

Stephen started the book in August 1982 and finished the first draft in 1983, but kept working on it until May 1987. He was drinking and doing drugs extensively during this period. In the introduction he says the book was "not so much written as gutted out." He recalled, "It was a hard one to write, just to keep track of all those people in the story and to make the story cohere. . . . I finally finished the rewrites and the whole process took about five years before I was happy with the book."[101]

The Tommyknockers was the last of four novels to be published in rapid succession. Stephen called it his "clearance sale" book and announced he was going on an extended sabbatical after it was published. At first, he suggested he might take five years off, but he softened that stance in subsequent interviews. He said he needed to recharge his batteries, that he was suffering from insomnia and headaches, and he felt like a conveyer belt producing books.

In fact, his family staged an intervention and Stephen began the process of getting clean during that period. Stephen later called *The Tommyknockers* an awful book. "That was the last one I wrote before I cleaned up my act. And I've thought about it a lot lately and said to myself, 'There's really a good book in here. . . . and I ought to go back.' The book is about 700 pages long, and I'm thinking, 'There's probably a good 350-page novel in there.'"[102]

THE DARK HALF (1989)

Anyone who has followed Stephen King's career will have no trouble figuring out his inspiration for *The Dark Half*. Even though he thought the Richard Bachman pen name had outlived its usefulness, he also had mixed feelings about the way in which his pseudonym had been exposed. It wasn't his choice: he was forced into admitting he had released five books under another name.

Stephen vented his frustration about that experience in this novel, creating a character named Frederick Clawson who attempts to blackmail his protagonist, Thad Beaumont. Clawson knows that while Beaumont has been publishing well-reviewed but poorly selling novels under his own name, he has also been releasing bestselling genre novels as George Stark.

OPPOSITE: Promotional poster for the 1993 miniseries based on *The Tommyknockers*.

Even though Stephen had declared Bachman dead, he occasionally had ideas that seemed better-suited to his alter ego. He felt Bachman was his darker, more violent side. "For a while I started to think, 'Suppose Bachman wasn't dead?' And immediately the idea jumped to mind: What if a guy had a pen name that didn't want to stay dead and isn't that an interesting idea and how would that work out?"[103]

When Stephen finished the first draft, he wasn't pleased with the result. "It just was flat and it had no shine to it. And one day I was driving along and all these sparrows took off in front of the car, and it was like this bright light went off in my head. I knew how that (device) would work and that it was what the book needed."[104]

Stephen was also troubled because he had no explanation for where George Stark came from. Simply wishing the make-believe person into existence wasn't enough. In an interview he said, "I went back to the idea of where personalities come from. It seems to me that every novel is an exercise in multiple personalities. The writer becomes several people at the same time and they talk to each other. . . . I started to play with the idea of multiple personalities and then I read somewhere . . . that sometimes twins are imperfectly absorbed in the womb and I thought, 'Now wait a minute. What if this guy is the ghost of a twin that never existed?' After that, I was able to wrap the whole book around that spine and it made everything a lot more coherent."[105]

OPPOSITE: British hardcover edition of *The Dark Half* from Hodder and Stoughton. ABOVE: Timothy Hutton as Thad Beaumont in the 1993 film adaptation of *The Dark Half*.

At first, he wanted to publish the book as a Bachman/King collaboration, but Viking didn't like the idea, feeling it might confuse readers, especially since he had just done an actual collaboration with Peter Straub. He also toyed with the idea of writing the novel George Stark was working on at the end of *The Dark Half*. "If I were to do that, it would be published as *Steel Machine* by Richard Bachman, not by George Stark. Because George Stark doesn't exist but Richard Bachman does."[106]

In the second introduction to *The Bachman Books*, he writes, "It's a book my wife has always hated, perhaps because, for Thad Beaumont, the dream of being a writer overwhelms the reality of being a man; for Thad, delusive thinking overtakes rationality completely, with horrific consequences."[107]

ADAPTATIONS

Hollywood discovered Stephen King in the 1980s, generating over a dozen cinematic adaptations during the decade. The first one, *The Shining* (1980), directed by Stanley Kubrick, opened to lackluster reviews despite high expectations. In subsequent decades, however, there has been a critical reevaluation of the movie, often deemed one of the best horror movies of all time. Stephen's dislike of the movie, though, is well-known. He has often been critical of it and ultimately decided to reacquire the rights so he could re-adapt it.

Stephen made his first appearance in a movie based on his work in *Creepshow* (1982), an anthology project based on two of his previously published short stories and three new ones, which Stephen scripted.

When the producers of the adaptation of *Cujo* (1983) asked Stephen if he would mind if they changed the ending to allow Tad Trenton to live, he did not object. "Movies aren't real," he explained.[108]

Another big-name director, David Cronenberg, adapted *The Dead Zone* (1983), still regarded as one of the best films made from a Stephen book.

Movie rights to *Christine* were acquired while the book was still in manuscript, and production began four days before the novel's publication date in 1983. The proximity of the film's premiere date to the book's release concerned his publishers, who feared it might impact book sales.

The most successful adaptation of the decade was Rob Reiner's version of *The Body*, known as *Stand by Me*. It was released the same year as Stephen's one and only directorial effort, *Maximum Overdrive* (based on his short story "Trucks"), which received far less critical acclaim.

By the end of the decade, a phenomenon began that would spread like wildfire in subsequent years—cinematic sequels, often only vaguely related to the original material.

See Appendix II for an extensive list of adaptations.

Gordie (Wil Wheaton), Chris (River Phoenix), Teddy (Corey Feldman), and Vern (Jerry O'Connell) from *Stand by Me*, Rob Reiner's adaptation of King's novella *The Body*.

CHAPTER 4

Experimentation and Change (1990s)

Now sober and after taking a short break from publishing, Stephen returned to the bestseller lists in the 1990s. The books he published in the early part of the decade were not always well-reviewed by critics, and Stephen occasionally admits that he considers some of those novels as failures. However, by the middle of the decade, he hit his stride again, publishing books that were both critically well-received and wildly popular.

Always looking for ways to expand his audience, Stephen experimented with new methods of publication. Toward the end of the decade, he ended his lengthy relationship with one publisher to work with another—a unique and revolutionary partnership that continues to this day.

THE STAND: THE COMPLETE & UNCUT EDITION (1990)

One of Stephen's long-time wishes was to see *The Stand* published in the form he had originally intended.

Discussions with Doubleday began as early as 1984; however, the publisher wasn't enthusiastic about the project. There were few other examples at the time of the release of an uncut edition of a previously published book. If they agreed to do it, Doubleday wouldn't promote the book as a major new work from Stephen and had no intention of trying to turn it into a bestseller.

Stephen added 250 pages to the book's original 823-page hardcover. How did he go about restoring the novel? He told the *New York Times*, "I actually sat down and wrote the book again. I had the manuscript on one side of an IBM Selectric typewriter and I had the pages of a book that I had torn out of the binding on the other side. And I started at the beginning and I updated the dates and wrote new material."[109] He didn't restore everything that had been previously deleted, though. Some of the original material belonged on the cutting-room floor, he decided.

In his preface to the new edition, part of which was meant to be read before potential buyers reached the cash register, Stephen warned readers, "This is not a brand-new, entirely different version of *The Stand*. You will not discover old characters behaving in new ways, nor will the course of the tale branch off at some point from the old narrative."[110]

Because Doubleday didn't think the restored edition would sell well, they decided to release it in May, a month when the publishing calendar looked quiet. Strong advance orders forced them to recalibrate, and they produced a first printing of at least 400,000 copies. Five days after its release, *The Stand: The Complete & Uncut Edition* entered the *New York Times* hardcover bestseller list at #1. By the end of 1990, the book had sold more than 700,000 copies.

FOUR PAST MIDNIGHT (1990)
*The Langoliers; Secret Window,
Secret Garden; The Library
Policeman; The Sun Dog*

During the two years of his so-called
break after writing *The Dark Half*,
Stephen worked on four novellas.
"I kept my hand in [writing]," he said.
"But I didn't work very hard. And it
was good."[111]

While his earlier novella collection,
Different Seasons, contained stories
that were mostly non-supernatural,
the four stories in *Four Past Midnight*
are darker and all contain horror
elements. In fact, Stephen was nervous
about this collection because people—
reviewers in particular—were going to compare it to that earlier collection. The
stories are longer than those in *Different Seasons* (most would be considered full
novels if written by anyone else) but, as he told the *Bangor Daily News*, "There's no
story like *The Body*. There'll just never be another story like that."[112]

The Langoliers was inspired by the image of a woman pressing her hand over a
crack in the wall of a commercial jetliner. As Stephen continued to dwell on the
image, he realized the woman was a ghost. He wrote the story in about a month
and says it was the one that came most easily of the four in the collection.

Stephen has had to withstand allegations of plagiarism several times during his
career. *Secret Window, Secret Garden* deals with a similar allegation made against its
protagonist. In his introduction to the story, Stephen said he thought it would be
the last time he wrote about writers and writing. Although he held to that belief for
several years, time would eventually prove him wrong about that.

The Library Policeman was inspired by Stephen's son Owen. He had told his
father he didn't like to use the library because he was still troubled by a story
his Aunt Stephanie had told him about the Library Police when he was younger.

Stephen thought the story would be humorous, but after about fifty pages "the whole story took a screaming left turn into the dark places I have travelled so often and which I still know so little about."[113]

The Sun Dog, which he intended to be the last of his *Castle Rock* stories, was inspired by Tabitha's interest in photography, which had started about five years earlier. She got a Polaroid camera and Stephen became fascinated with the images it produced. "The more I thought about them, the stranger they seemed. They are, after all, not just images but moments of time . . . and there is something so peculiar about them."[114]

NEEDFUL THINGS (1991)

While he was revisiting *The Stand*, Stephen was also preparing to bring one of his longstanding creations to an end. Billed as "The Last Castle Rock Story," *Needful Things* wasn't only meant to be the end of his fictional town, it was intended to represent a change in direction, "the finish of a lot of old business," he said.[115] Stephen was beginning to believe that being typecast as a horror writer was becoming a burden. *Needful Things* was meant to be his last supernatural horror novel. He said, "It is time to be done with Castle Rock because it is too easy to keep coming back to it. Too easy to rehash all the things which have occurred there over the years—the rabid dog, the crazy cop, those kids who ended a summer in search of a dead body along some railroad tracks."[116]

OPPOSITE: British hardcover edition of *Four Past Midnight* from Hodder and Stoughton. RIGHT: Movie poster for the 1993 movie adaptation of *Needful Things* featuring Ed Harris as Sheriff Alan Pangborn and Bonnie Bedelia as Polly Chalmers.

Stephen wanted to write a story about obsessive and compulsive behavior. "The idea for that book came all at once. I thought, 'What if somebody came to this town and forced all these people to do nasty things like pranks [to each other] to get things that they really wanted.'"[117] He told *Fangoria*, "For a long time, I worked with just simply one image . . . a little boy throwing mud at sheets. And I knew that whoever came home and discovered the mud on the sheets was going to think somebody else did it."[118] He believed readers would think a book about people willing to sell their souls to buy something was funny."[119]

"For me, *Needful Things* was the most fun I ever had with a novel," he told Fangoria. "It's got a huge cast. It's a throwback to some of the things like *'Salem's Lot* and *The Stand* where I threw in fifty or sixty characters and then...threw in thirty more. . . . This is like Stephen King's greatest hits, man. Even *Cujo* is back."[120] But by 2006, Stephen had reevaluated the book. "The reviewers called it an unsuccessful horror novel, even though I had assumed everybody would see it as a satire. Over the years I've come to think that, well, maybe it just wasn't a very good book."[121]

GERALD'S GAME (1992) AND DOLORES CLAIBORNE (1992)

Stephen wanted to take the summer of 1990 off from writing before starting *Dolores Claiborne* that fall. The book had already been announced for 1992 publication. However, his artistic inspiration had other plans. While on a flight to New York, he fell asleep and dreamed about a woman handcuffed to a bed.

"I said: 'Oh, that's wonderful, what a great idea. I must write it.' Not because it was a whole story but because it was one of these situations that's so interesting that you figure if you start to write it, things will suggest themselves. So I worked on it and I complained to my wife a lot about it, because I had not wanted to write last summer. I just wanted to sort of play baseball and goof off, and that isn't the way it turned out."[122]

The end result was *Gerald's Game*, a book which, if his pseudonym hadn't passed away, might have been published under the name Richard Bachman. What the dream didn't tell him was how to get his protagonist out of her predicament. He enlisted the help of his son Joe to test one of his ideas for resolving the problem, but it didn't work.

Dolores Claiborne was pushed back, but he eventually returned to his idea about a woman who spends the entire novel confessing to murdering her husband. Writing a book where the main character is an older woman was something new for Stephen. He based the character on his mother and named her Dolores because it "means

A scene from the 1995 feature adaptation of *Dolores Claiborne* starring Kathy Bates and Jennifer Jason Leigh.

sadness or sorrow, and that's appropriate to the kind of life that she's led."[123] These would be the first two of a trio of books Stephen would write in the 1990s featuring female protagonists who are victims of male oppression, but symbols of female empowerment at the same time. "It went back to that thing of being interested in women and wanting to try and do away with the male protagonist for a while and go back to where I was at the beginning with *Carrie*, only to try and do it better, with a little more maturity. . . . I'd like to think I'm doing some things better or thinking a little more clearly or even that experience has just taught me some things."[124]

Gerald's Game and *Dolores Claiborne* are linked by a scene that takes place during a solar eclipse. There has long been a rumor they were originally written as a single book called *In the Path of the Eclipse* and Stephen was encouraged by his publisher to separate them. Stephen clarifies the situation: "I thought for a while that I could put the two together and [release] them as one volume. . . . But these things were a little bit longer and just would not be harnessed together. So eventually I decided to do them separately."[125]

NIGHTMARES & DREAMSCAPES (1993)

"Dolan's Cadillac," "The End of the Whole Mess," "Suffer the Little Children," "The Night Flier," "Popsy," "It Grows on You," "Chattery Teeth," "Dedication," "The Moving Finger," "Sneakers," "You Know They Got a Hell of a Band," "Home Delivery," "Rainy Season," "My Pretty Pony," "Sorry, Right Number," "The Ten O'Clock People," "Crouch End," "The House on Maple Street," "The Fifth Quarter," "The Doctor's Case," "Umney's Last Case," "Head Down," "Brooklyn August," "The Beggar and the Diamond"

In the introduction to Stephen's 1993 collection *Nightmares & Dreamscapes*, he says he had been finding it difficult to write short stories lately. "These days it seems that everything wants to be a novel, and every novel wants to be approximately four thousand pages long."[126] Stephen says this book collects all the existing stories he considers good enough to be republished. "All the bad ones have been swept as far under the rug as I could get them, and there they will stay. If there is to be another collection, it will consist entirely of stories which have not as yet been written or even considered."[127]

The oldest story in the collection dated back to his college years. The book includes three previously unpublished stories, a poem, a parable, a teleplay, and an essay from the *New Yorker*, along with extensive story notes. Shortly before *Nightmares & Dreamscapes* was published, one of its stories, "Umney's Last Case," was made available as an e-book—the first time Stephen was published electronically.

INSOMNIA (1994)

Stephen's next two novels have taken some of his sharpest self-criticism in later years. He says the books are overly plot-driven and "the results have not been particularly inspiring."[128] He felt he had forced the books to go in a particular direction to get to the ending he wanted. In one case, he wouldn't let a character do something the character wanted to do, which resulted in a story that was tough for him to believe. He told *Time* magazine ". . . if I can't believe some of these things, I can't expect readers to believe them because, let's face it, they're pretty out there anyway."[129]

Stephen has long suffered from insomnia, so it's only natural that at some point he would use that affliction in a novel. He told attendees of an online chat[130] he barely slept during the four months he was working on *Insomnia* in 1990. In a 1992 interview, he deemed the 550-page manuscript unpublishable. "The thing that hurts is that the last eighty or ninety pages are wonderful. But things just don't connect, it doesn't have that novelistic roundness that it should have. And maybe some day you'll read it, but it won't be for a long time."[131]

Stephen came up with an interesting idea for his promotional tour for the book. He appeared at ten independent bookstores, traveling from Vermont to California on his Harley-Davidson motorcycle, a 4,690-mile trip that became part of his novel, *Desperation*.

ROSE MADDER (1995)

Stephen's inspiration for *Rose Madder* was a news story about a woman who had been shot by her husband, even though she had a protection order against him.

He later came to judge the book as one of his "stiff, trying-too-hard novels."[132] In an interview, he said, "I had a terrific idea going into that book. And it just kind of shriveled on me, and I kept pushing. And I published the book and it didn't get very good reviews. And it didn't deserve to get good reviews, because it felt like something that had been shoved through the door."[133]

Stephen felt the reason the book was worth writing was for the protagonist's discovery at the end that, even though she had settled matters with her abusive husband, she's not done being angry. "That's what happens to us. . . . You get angry enough at somebody, if you're terrorized enough, you grow a tree of your own rage and then what are you going to do about it? How are you going to get rid of it?"[134]

AUDIO KING

Virtually all of Stephen's novels are available in unabridged audio versions. He recorded the audio versions of the first three *Dark Tower* novels himself, making use of the studio at WZON, the radio station he owns in Bangor. Careful listeners can hear traffic sounds in the background of these early recordings. For subsequent books in the series, professional narrators were hired, although Stephen himself recorded *The Wind Through the Keyhole*, and has narrated a number of his other books and stories.

STEPHEN KING

THE GREEN MILE

THE COMPLETE SERIAL NOVEL

Scribner's hardcover edition, released four years after *The Green Mile* first appeared in monthly installments.

THE GREEN MILE (1996)

Stephen had been working on a story called "What Tricks Your Eye," about a huge Black man on death row "who develops an interest in sleight-of-hand as the date for his execution draws near. The story was to be told in the first person, by an old trusty who wheeled a cart of books through the cell blocks. . . . At the end of the story, just before his execution, I wanted the huge prisoner, Luke Coffey, to make himself disappear."[135]

He worked on the story in his mind while struggling with insomnia. Each night he would add a little bit more before finally falling asleep. Usually he got tired of these "cure for insomnia" stories and started a new one after a while. This story stuck with him longer than most, but he couldn't get it to work until a year and a half later, when he came up with a different slant: "Suppose . . . the big guy was a healer of some sort instead of an aspiring magician . . . condemned for murders that he not only did not commit but had tried to reverse?"[136]

As promising as the idea seemed, Stephen was too busy to write it. He remembers, "I had filled a notebook with scribbled pages . . . and realized I was building a novel when I should have been spending my time clearing my desk for revisions on [*Desperation*]."[137] He was about to abandon the story when his foreign rights agent came to him with a suggestion.

The agent and a British editor had been discussing serial publications. For example, Charles Dickens's works were published in installments in the nineteenth century. The editor wondered whether it would be possible to produce a book in cheap installments in the twentieth century. The two men agreed Stephen was probably the only living author whom publishers would risk releasing a book in sections while he was still writing it.

The agent's suggestion gave Stephen the excuse he needed to set aside time to write the death row novel that became *The Green Mile*. It would be a fascinating process, particularly because he had not yet written the last installment when the first one appeared. He reveled in the danger of the approach, saying, "I liked the high-wire aspect of it, too: fall down on the job, fail to carry through, and all at once about a million readers are howling for your blood."[138]

Stephen "wrote like a madman" to keep up with the publishing schedule, sometimes afraid he was making the biggest mistake of his life. His work was complicated by the requirement that each installment be the same length and end with a mini-climax. He also didn't have the luxury of backing up to change details if the story went in a different direction. He said there was "less margin for screwing up—it had to be right the first time."[139]

The Green Mile takes place on E Block in Cold Mountain State Penitentiary in 1932 in an unspecified Southern state. As a framing device, Stephen establishes a first-person narrator, Paul Edgecombe, the former block supervisor, who is recounting those long-ago events from a Georgia nursing home. E Block is the place where prisoners await their date with the electric chair. Stephen says, "'Old Sparky' has fascinated me ever since . . . the first Death Row tales I ever read . . . fired the darker side of my imagination. What, I wondered, would it be like to walk those last forty yards to the electric chair, knowing you were going to die there? What, for that matter, would it be like to be the man who had to strap the condemned in . . . or pull the switch? What would such a job take out of you?"[140]

The lives of the guardians of E Block are complicated by the introduction of a gentle giant, a simple man accused of the brutal murders of two young girls. He was found with the dead girls in his lap, and his statement upon arrest seemed to acknowledge his guilt. The character Stephen first called Luke Coffey became John Coffey, and his touch could heal. "I decided to give him the initials J.C., after the most famous innocent man of all time," Stephen said. "I wasn't sure, right up to the end of the book, if my J.C. would live or die. I wanted him to live because I liked and pitied him, but I figured those initials couldn't hurt, one way or the other."[141]

Understandably, some readers drew conclusions about King's personal beliefs about the death penalty, but he counters, "I think there's an assumption, based on the book, that I'm against the death penalty. I'm not.... I believe it should be an absolute last resort."[142]

The book's villains aren't the convicted killers on Death Row—except, perhaps, for William "Billy the Kid" Wharton, who is truly heinous. The villain in the piece is a system that treats everyone subject to it the same way and has no mechanism for compassion. Percy Wetmore is the embodiment of this system, a cruel, ambitious guard who has influential connections that guarantee his position on E Block.

Though *The Green Mile* is ultimately a tragedy, a sense of optimism pervades it. John Coffey's heroism and compassion touch everyone he encounters during his stay on E Block—and especially during one unauthorized night journey to the warden's house to cure his wife's cancer. Seventy years later, Paul Edgecombe is a living

King sits in the electric chair on the set of *The Green Mile*, with director Frank Darabont (left) and star Tom Hanks.

testament to Coffey's lasting gift, although it is an open question whether Paul's longevity is a boon or a curse.

The book's release was a logistical nightmare. For six consecutive months, the publisher had to orchestrate the delivery and release of each installment on a specific date, a rare occurrence in paperback publishing. Booksellers were asked to sign documents binding them to the agreed-upon release dates for the books, to prevent them from going on sale early. The publisher's worst nightmare was that eager sellers would buy far too many copies of the first installment. Because of the way paperback returns are handled, the numbers wouldn't filter back to the publisher in time to adjust the print runs for subsequent installments.

They needn't have worried. The book and its unique delivery system were both a critical and a publishing success. The fact that each installment went on sale on the same day across the continent—and also in translation in a number of other countries worldwide—meant that everyone was experiencing the story at the same rate. No one could "read ahead" and spoil the ending—for themself or for anyone else. Online message boards were alive with discussion about the story and its intriguing characters, speculating about what would happen next month. Stephen's publisher fanned interest by taking advantage of the internet. Their website offered contests where readers could win prizes. They created a serial screensaver for computers that expanded along with the book. TV advertisements were also made available on the website. From March through August 1996, *The Green Mile* was the focus of attention of Stephen fans and the publishing industry alike.

Part I, *The Two Dead Girls*, went straight to the top of the bestseller list, as did each subsequent installment of the serial. Eighteen million copies of the booklets ended up in print and Stephen set a world record for having the most books on the bestseller list simultaneously in September 1996, when all six installments were on *The New York Times* list—a phenomenon that triggered a change in the way future serialized books would be classified on the list.

Tom Hanks and Michael Clarke Duncan in a scene from the 1999 film adaptation of *The Green Mile*.

DESPERATION (1996) AND *THE REGULATORS* (1996)

In 1991, while Stephen was driving cross-country, he passed through Ruth, Nevada, apparent population: zero. He immediately thought everyone must be dead, followed by the question—if that's the case, who killed them? His answer: "The sheriff killed them all. And when an answer comes back that quickly, there's a book there."[143] Stephen made a second stop at Ruth on his motorcycle during his promotional tour for *Insomnia*. "The other thing that's interested me ever since I was a kid was the idea . . . that God is cruel," Stephen said.[144] "I really wanted to give God his due in this book. So often, in novels of the supernatural, God is a sort of kryptonite substance, or like holy water to a vampire. You just bring on God, and you say 'in his name,' and the evil thing disappears. But God as a real force in human lives is a lot more complex than that. And I wanted to say that in *Desperation*. God doesn't always let the good guys win."[145]

When he was about three-quarters of the way through *Desperation*, another idea came to him. He wrote the word "Regulators" on a scrap of paper and taped it to the side of his printer as a reminder. On another day, inspiration struck—he would take characters from *Desperation* and put them into this new novel. "In some cases, I thought, they could play the same people; in others, they would change; in neither would they do the same things or react in the same ways, because the different stories would dictate different courses of action. It would be, I thought, like the members of a repertory company acting in two different plays."[146]

The final piece to the puzzle fell into place when he decided to have Richard Bachman write *The Regulators*. "I didn't actually bring Richard Bachman back from the dead, anyway; I just visualized a box of neglected manuscripts in the basement, with *The Regulators* on top. Then I transcribed the book Bachman had already written."[147] He started writing *The Regulators* the day after he finished *Desperation*.

The two books were published on the same day one month after the final installment of *The Green Mile* hit bookshelves, issued by two different publishers (Viking and Dutton). Some copies were bundled with a night-light to encourage people to buy both. When the novels were placed side by side, the cover art formed a larger image. Dutton wanted to attribute *The Regulators* to "Stephen King writing as Richard Bachman," but Stephen refused.

It was a big year for Viking, with the promise of a new installment in the *Dark Tower* series in the coming months. However, it was to be Stephen's last year with them. After nearly two decades, he decided it was time for a fresh start.

BAG OF BONES (1998)

Shortly after the miniseries version of *The Shining* aired on television, Stephen decided to take a rare overseas vacation, riding his motorcycle across the Australian plains.

While he was away, a firestorm swept through the publishing world. News emerged that Stephen had reached an impasse in contract negotiations with his current publisher, and his next manuscript was up for bid. "I had gotten a bit stale at Viking, and we had reached a point where we were a bit too comfortable with each other," Stephen says.[148]

When popular authors are involved in contract negotiations at this level, auctions are usually confidential. In this case, however, Stephen's attorney sent queries to several publishers simultaneously, and when news leaked out, the process quickly made headlines. One publisher was quoted as saying he thought the letter was a joke being played on him by a friend, but it was no joke. Stephen's lawyer started meeting with interested parties. Stephen later regretted that the search for a new publisher attracted so much publicity.

Advances for big-name authors like Stephen had reached levels where the books were no longer profitable for the publisher. Ultimately, an unusual agreement was reached with Scribner to publish Stephen's next three books. His advance would be a relatively modest $2 million, but his share of royalties would be much greater. If a book did well, his publisher and he both benefited. If a book didn't meet expectations, the publisher wouldn't be on the hook for a major loss.

Stephen's first novel to be published under the Scribner imprint was *Bag of Bones*. To prepare for its marketing

King during his 1997 motorcycle trip across Australia.

campaign, Scribner conducted focus groups to identify readers who had fallen away from Stephen and those who knew of his works only through film adaptations. They downplayed the horror aspect and played up the book's literary and romantic sides.

Stephen's perspective was: "I wanted to write a gothic novel, and for me that is a novel about secrets. About things that happened in the past that have been buried and stay quiet for a while, and then, like a buried body, they start to smell bad. . . . I love the idea of secrets and secrets always find their way out."[149]

Bag of Bones is the story of moderately successful novelist Mike Noonan, who has reached a plateau in his career. Early in the book, his wife, Jo, dies of a catastrophic stroke in the parking lot of a Derry pharmacy. Among the items in her shopping bag: a home pregnancy test. Mike and Jo have been trying to have a child for years, so the pregnancy test comes as a surprise to Mike. It makes him wonder what other secrets his late wife might have been keeping from him.

One of the strange and lingering effects of his new status as a widower is that Mike acquires the world's worst case of writer's block. He keeps this a secret from everyone, including his agent and his publisher. "Mike is probably as close as you could get to me," Stephen says, "even though I've been careful to distance myself from him. . . . our take on what writing is about and how the writing works is very similar."[150] Shortly after the book was released, Stephen joked, "There are probably a few critics out there who wish I had a little more writer's block."

Mike can afford to hide his writer's block. Although he has published a book a year for the past decade, during four of those years he wrote two books, so he has four manuscripts squirreled away in a safety deposit box. All he needs to do to keep his modest publishing career in motion is to make an annual withdrawal from the vault. Mike is amused when his editor tells him he's taken his work to the next level, not realizing she's discussing a manuscript he wrote over a decade ago.

Readers wondered if Stephen had manuscripts stockpiled, too, but that wasn't the case. That detail was inspired by a rumor about a romance writer who was supposedly writing three books a year but only publishing two. "If that's true over the last ten years, she must have a lot piled up," he said.[151]

The root of Mike's problem is that he's afraid of moving ahead with life without his spouse. If he starts writing again, everything he had with Jo might unravel. He stays in Derry for the next four years, spending most of his free time playing Scrabble and doing crossword puzzles on his computer. He compares himself to the English novelist and poet Thomas Hardy, who gave up writing books, and thinks of himself as a bag of bones, which is how Hardy supposedly described characters in novels.

At night, Mike dreams of Sara Laughs, the Noonans' summer home on Dark Score Lake in western Maine. These dreams remind him of the opening line of Daphne du Maurier's novel *Rebecca*: "Last night I dreamt I went to Manderley again." Despite his dreams, it never occurs to Mike to go there. His dreams change subtly over time, as if the house is beckoning to him. At the same time, he feels like something dangerous is waiting for him there.

When his final book from the vault really catches his publisher's interest and they want to open negotiations for a new multi-book contract worth millions of dollars, Mike decides to get away. He can't explain his dilemma to anyone. He decides to take an acquaintance's advice and plans a vacation to the summer house. Stephen says, "Suppose the narrator finds out that his wife was involved with a lot of things he didn't know about, and he comes back to this place suspecting she was there and discovers something else entirely."[152]

Shortly after Mike arrives, several things happen that change his life. First, he believes Sara Laughs is haunted—perhaps by the ghost of his late wife. He starts receiving messages, spelled out with refrigerator magnets, for example. He also senses a presence while exploring the house for clues about his wife's activities.

Interviewers often ask Stephen if he has ever written anything that frightened him. Although he usually says no, he admits that part of *Bag of Bones* has had a lasting effect. He describes the scene in detail: "Mike Noonan goes downstairs to look for something in the cellar, and the door shuts behind him, and something begins to thump on the wall insulation. And he realizes he's with a spirit he can talk to by asking 'yes' or 'no' questions, and the thing will thump once for 'yes' and twice for 'no.' And I found myself visualizing our stairway in our home, which has insulation on the walls. . . . So that now, whenever I go down the stairwell, I'm immediately reminded of that scene in the book, and I'm afraid that the door's going to swing shut behind me and the lights are going to go out and something's going to start thumping on the wall."[153]

Mike also acquires a love interest and a cause. While driving to lunch one day, he narrowly misses hitting a little girl on the side of Route 68. A few minutes later he meets the girl's distraught mother—Mattie Devore, a single mother who he immediately dismisses as trailer trash. However, his first impression is quickly overturned, and

STEPHEN KING

BAG OF BONES

A NOVEL

THE INNOVATOR

Over the years, Stephen has experimented with nontraditional forms of publication.

In 1993, he made his short story "Umney's Last Case" available over the internet several weeks prior to its appearance in *Nightmares & Dreamscapes*. This was before web browsers were a fixture of every home computer. People who paid a $5 fee could use an FTP service to log into a remote computer and download the story, which came bundled with a program that displayed the text onscreen.

In 1996, Stephen breathed new life into the serial novel with his six-month release of *The Green Mile*. Several other authors attempted to duplicate his success in that format, but none came close.

His next experiment in digital release was the novella *Riding the Bullet*, written after his accident. All these years later, it's hard to appreciate how revolutionary this was at the time. The entire publishing industry was watching to see what happened when it went on sale for $2.50, with some retailers offering it for free. Over 400,000 copies were reportedly sold the first day alone, and the number might have been higher if demand hadn't caused systems to slow to a crawl or crash. Analysts estimated that, while Stephen might have made $10,000 for the story in a print magazine, he stood to earn nearly half a million dollars from downloads.

With *The Plant*, Stephen tested the theory that most people are honest. Six installments of the novel-in-progress were made available on his website on the honor system. If a large-enough percentage of people who downloaded the files contributed a dollar, he promised to continue with the project. Before the numbers were tallied, though, Stephen discovered the story wasn't working for him and abandoned the project.

From short stories and novel fragments, he moved on to the world of electronic books. *The Girl Who Loved Tom Gordon* was his first e-book, released in 1999. That same year, a screensaver bundle was issued with these (at the time) innovative features: six screensavers (called Screamsavers) and interactive mini-games, a trivia game, the entire text of the novella *Everything's Eventual*, and customizable desktop images with blood-curdling sound files.

He released the novella *Ur* exclusively for—and inspired by—the Kindle book reader. To promote *Cell*, the publisher encouraged people to sign up for text alerts and purchase cell phone wallpapers and ringtones.

he finds himself attracted to someone barely half his age. "Here's a guy that's been grieving for four years," Stephen explains. "It's been raining in his life for four years. And she's the first ray of sunshine that he sees."[154] She's young and beautiful, but also vulnerable. Mattie's husband was killed in a freak accident and her wealthy father-in-law is trying to get custody of her daughter, Kyra. Enough people witnessed the incident on the side of the road that it provides testimony against Mattie's mothering skills. Mike decides to help Mattie, using his considerable savings to fund her legal battle. As he falls in love, he comes to life again. He even starts to write. At first, he thinks the secret to solving his block was getting away from his computer and working at an old electric IBM typewriter, but there's more going on than that. The spirits in the basement, who inspire his novels, have a message they're trying to convey on behalf of someone else, coded into his new manuscript. He starts to wonder if ghosts can be crazy—if a person's essence might survive, but without its sanity intact.

After unraveling a complex tale of a past crime that has been covered up for generations, Mike Noonan decides to quit writing for good. "I've lost my taste for spooks . . . I've put down my . . . pen." Many readers saw this as Stephen's official notice of his intent to retire, or to at least change gears. Stephen himself said, "As I began work on *Bag of Bones*, I looked a few sheets down the calendar and saw fifty staring me in the face."[155] In fact, it was something of a new beginning for Stephen—the start of critical acceptance for his work.

THE GIRL WHO LOVED TOM GORDON (1999)

Stephen took Scribner by surprise when he delivered the manuscript for a novella about a young girl who is a baseball fan. She gets lost in the woods and relies on her imaginary connection with her favorite player, a relief pitcher named Tom Gordon who was used to high-pressure situations. "The idea of closing a ballgame began to merge in my mind with the idea of this girl being lost in the woods," Stephen said.[156]

Famously a fan of the Boston Red Sox, Stephen saw something that inspired him to use a real-life person in his story. "I started to notice that Tom points to the sky when he finishes a ballgame, which to me says, 'I saved the game by the grace of God.' Since I wanted to say something about God in this book, Tom seemed like the perfect person for this girl to have as her hero."[157]

The novella was originally conceived as a short story but turned into something much longer. "I never thought much about the name issue until it grew into a novel.

At that point I figured I'd better get in touch with Tom and see if it would be all right."[158]

The story is set in June 1998, the summer when Gordon set a major-league record for consecutive saves. What did the Red Sox pitcher think about his appearance in the novella? "For a man like Stephen King to do something like this is truly a blessing to me and my family. It's all my family is talking about. . . . I'm just grateful it was Stephen King doing this and not somebody pulling a prank."[159]

The Girl Who Loved Tom Gordon was released on opening day for Major League Baseball, April 6, 1999. It was Stephen's first book to be simultaneously released as an e-book. Stephen told a reporter the book was not a lucky one for Gordon or himself.[160] He'd thrown the first pitch at Fenway Park at a game where Gordon was injured while pitching. Two weeks later, Stephen was struck by a minivan, an accident that permanently altered his life.

HEARTS IN ATLANTIS (1999)
Hearts in Atlantis, Low Men in Yellow Coats, "Blind Willie," "Why We're in Vietman," "Heavenly Shades of Night are Falling"

When Stephen signed his three-book deal with Scribner, one of the books he intended to be included was a short story collection. His muse had other ideas.

While revising *Bag of Bones*, he wrote a novella called *Hearts in Atlantis*. It was the right length for a book like *Different Seasons*, but he didn't have any other stories of similar length to go with it. He ended up combining *Hearts in Atlantis* with one other novella and three short stories.

Although Stephen was a university student during much of the Vietnam war, he hadn't explored his thoughts about that era in his fiction. In a promo letter from Scribner, Stephen writes, "I was . . . drawing on an incident I observed when still a freshman in college. I had no particular plans to publish the story, but I thought it might amuse my kids. And that was how I found my way in. I began to see a way I might be able to write about what we almost had, what we lost, and what we finally ended up with, and how to do it without preaching."[161] The main character, Pete

Riley, is a reasonable representation of Stephen, who says he underwent a profound political awakening as a college student.

Next, he wrote *Low Men in Yellow Coats*, returning to memories of his childhood. "The building where Bobby lives is the building where I lived when I was his age, and the details, the geography are all the same," Stephen says.[162] This story also ties in with the *Dark Tower* series.

Hearts in Atlantis is an interesting hybrid—not quite a novel but more than a collection. The stories "kind of revolve around that Vietnam experience. Not about the war itself, but more about how the war influenced American thought and the way that we behave," Stephen said.[163]

ADAPTATIONS

The 1990s demonstrated the full spectrum of what is possible in adapting Stephen's work. Some of the most popular and celebrated movies based on his work appeared in this decade, films like *Misery*, *The Shawshank Redemption*, and *The Green Mile*.

The direct-to-video revolution that started in the late 1980s created a market for a stream of "sequels" to short-story-based movies like *Children of the Corn* (four in the 1990s alone, with more to come), *Sometimes They Come Back*, and *The Mangler*.

Some of the lower-budget movies were decent, though. Mick Garris directed *Sleepwalkers*, based on King's original script, and *The Night Flier* was an effective vampire film based on a short story.

The 1990s also saw the production of several miniseries based on Stephen's work, including two series (*Golden Years* and *Storm of the Century*) written specifically for television. King was also directly involved in the production of miniseries based on *The Stand* and *The Shining*.

See Appendix II for an extensive list of adaptations.

Photo booth pictures of King taken in the late 1960s.

THE ACCIDENT

On June 19, 1999, Stephen made the long, slow drive along Maine's country roads to Portland, where he dropped his son Owen off at the airport. The rest of the family was planning to go to a movie in New Hampshire that evening, but Stephen had time after he returned home for a nap and his traditional afternoon four-mile walk.

As usual, Stephen was reading during his walk. However, when he reached a short, steep hill with poor sight lines, he lowered the book so he could watch for oncoming traffic. He remembers what happened next clearly: "I was three-quarters of the way up this hill when Bryan Smith, the owner and operator of the Dodge van, came over the crest. He wasn't on the road; he was on the shoulder. My shoulder. I had perhaps three-quarters of a second to register this."[164]

Bryan Smith had a cooler behind him in his van, and his Rottweiler, Bullet, was nosing at it, trying to get at the raw meat inside. Smith ignored the road and turned to scold the dog. The van drifted onto the shoulder, making a beeline for Stephen, who turned slightly at the last minute—an instinctive move that probably saved his life.[165]

One of the most chilling indications of the force of the impact is the fact that Stephen's eyeglasses ended up on the front seat of Smith's van. King later wrote, "It occurs to me that I have nearly been killed by a character right out of one of my own novels. It's almost funny."

Stephen's injuries were severe. While being transported to the hospital, his lung collapsed. One leg was so badly broken below the knee that a doctor described the bones as being like "marbles in a sock." His knee was split down the middle and his hip was fractured in two places. His spine was chipped in eight places and four ribs were broken. The flesh above his collarbone was stripped raw, and he required twenty or thirty stitches to close a laceration in his scalp.

After a week of complicated procedures to insert pins and rods into his leg, he was finally able to get out of bed for the first time. This was just the beginning of his ordeal, though. For someone with Stephen's addiction history, dealing with powerful pain medication was a challenge. He had been sober for over a decade. Stephen recounts that he took the Oxycontin he had been prescribed until he didn't need it anymore. However, the addictive part of him began creating pain so that he could get more of the drug. He ultimately realized that he needed to stop taking it. It was a difficult process, but he did it.

Two weeks after the accident, he was able to sit up in a wheelchair for the first time. A week after that, he was allowed to return home, where he underwent a daily rehab program to rebuild strength and mobility in his crushed leg. In August, he had surgery to remove the pins that protruded from his upper thigh.

News of Stephen's accident spread quickly. While the response was generally sympathetic, his popularity made him an obvious target for the late-night talk-show hosts. They made jokes about how many books he had written while in the hospital, but to Stephen, these jokes were not the least bit funny. He was truly worried he might never be able to write again—that the chronic pain he would suffer for the rest of his life would destroy any creative impulses within him. "But without even thinking about it, I had written an account of the accident probably three days after I came out of the anesthesia. And that was fairly complete. And I didn't do it because anybody asked me to. I did it because I wanted to put down on paper what I remembered. So as soon as I could hold a pen, I was writing."[166]

Stephen had ample reason not to write. He was restricted to a walker and couldn't sit up for long periods of time. However, when he decided he wanted to go back to work, Tabitha immediately supported the idea and spent part of an afternoon setting up a temporary office for him. "Tabitha ... knows when I'm working too hard, but she also knows that sometimes it's the work that bails me out," he wrote in *On Writing*.[167]

Writing has always been the one constant in Stephen's life, and during this personal crisis it was the best cure for his pain. He said it was "very difficult to push the pen forty-five minutes a day, but it was vital to get back to work, because you have to break the ice somehow. You have to say, 'This is what I do.' I'm either going to continue to work, or I'm not. You say, 'If I can do this, maybe I can walk. If I can walk, maybe I can resume some kind of human intercourse.' Work seemed like a logical place to start."[168]

Stephen's work after his accident was frequently inspired by the experience. For example, it became a central part of the *Dark Tower* series. There is a popular belief that true art arises from misery or suffering. Whether or not that is the case, Stephen's muses were definitely influenced by the trauma he endured in 1999—and the pain he has suffered ever since.

MOVIE STAR

In 1985, Stephen agreed to film a commercial that featured him wearing a smoking jacket and carrying a candle as he walks through a haunted house. "Do you know me?" he asked. "It's frightening how many novels of suspense I've written. But still, when I'm not recognized, it just kills me. So instead of saying I wrote *Carrie*, I carry the American Express card. Without it, life's a little scary."[169]

That wasn't his first time in front of the movie camera. His big-screen debut was in 1981 in the movie, *Knightriders*, where Stephen and Tabitha play a couple of hecklers in the crowd. He played the title character in one of the five segments of the 1982 movie *Creepshow*, which also featured a very young Joe King as the boy whose father throws away his horror comic books. Stephen's other film and television appearances have mostly been cameos in adaptations of his novels and short stories, usually playing humorous characters.

Stephen was also invited to appear in an episode of *Sons of Anarchy*, in which he plays a "fixer" named Bachman, he was a caller on an episode of *Frasier*, and he was animated on an episode of *The Simpsons*.

Stephen has also appeared on *Celebrity Jeopardy* twice, in 1995 and in 1998. A conversation with David Duchovny during his first appearance led to him writing an episode of *The X-Files*.

CHAPTER 5

After the Accident (2000s)

There is no question that Stephen's accident had a huge impact on his life—both personally and professionally. Although he recovered from the worst of his injuries, he continued to suffer after-effects, some of them life-threatening.

Characters suffering serious physical injuries began to appear regularly in his books and stories, and the fact that he wrote frequently about pain reveals much about what he was enduring during this decade and beyond.

However, the books he wrote for Scribner received far more favorable critical attention than his earlier novels, and the literary establishment began to re-evaluate Stephen's career. One book in particular is often praised even by people who don't regularly read his novels: his deeply personal book about the art of writing.

ON WRITING (2000)

Stephen began *On Writing* at the end of 1997, but put it aside a few months later, unsure how to finish it. Over a year later, in mid-1999, he decided to spend the summer "finishing the damn writing book."[170] His accident derailed those plans, but in late July, when he decided it was time to start writing again, he chose *On Writing* for his first project. He was interested in exploring questions never asked of popular novelists, including how much writers like him care about the art and craft of telling stories and their attention to language.

Stephen is more revealing about his life in this book than ever before. He addresses his battle with alcohol and drug abuse, when it started, how it evolved, and how he was eventually forced to confront his problem. He also frankly discusses the merits and deficiencies of many of his books.

In the sections about writing, Stephen describes his writer's toolbox and his taboos. He emphasizes the importance of reading for anyone who wants to be a writer, and he recommends having a place with a door that a writer is willing to shut while working. He includes examples of both good and bad writing, sometimes taken from his own work. He also describes his approach to research.

Toward the end of the book, Stephen tackles the subject of his accident. Throughout the book, but especially in "On Living: A Postscript," Stephen pays tribute to wife, Tabitha. She is Stephen's "Ideal Reader," the person for whom he writes all his books, the one who he wants to make laugh or cry through his writing. His love and admiration for her shines through, from their early courtship to her organization of a group intervention to make him confront his addiction and her support and encouragement of him during his recovery.

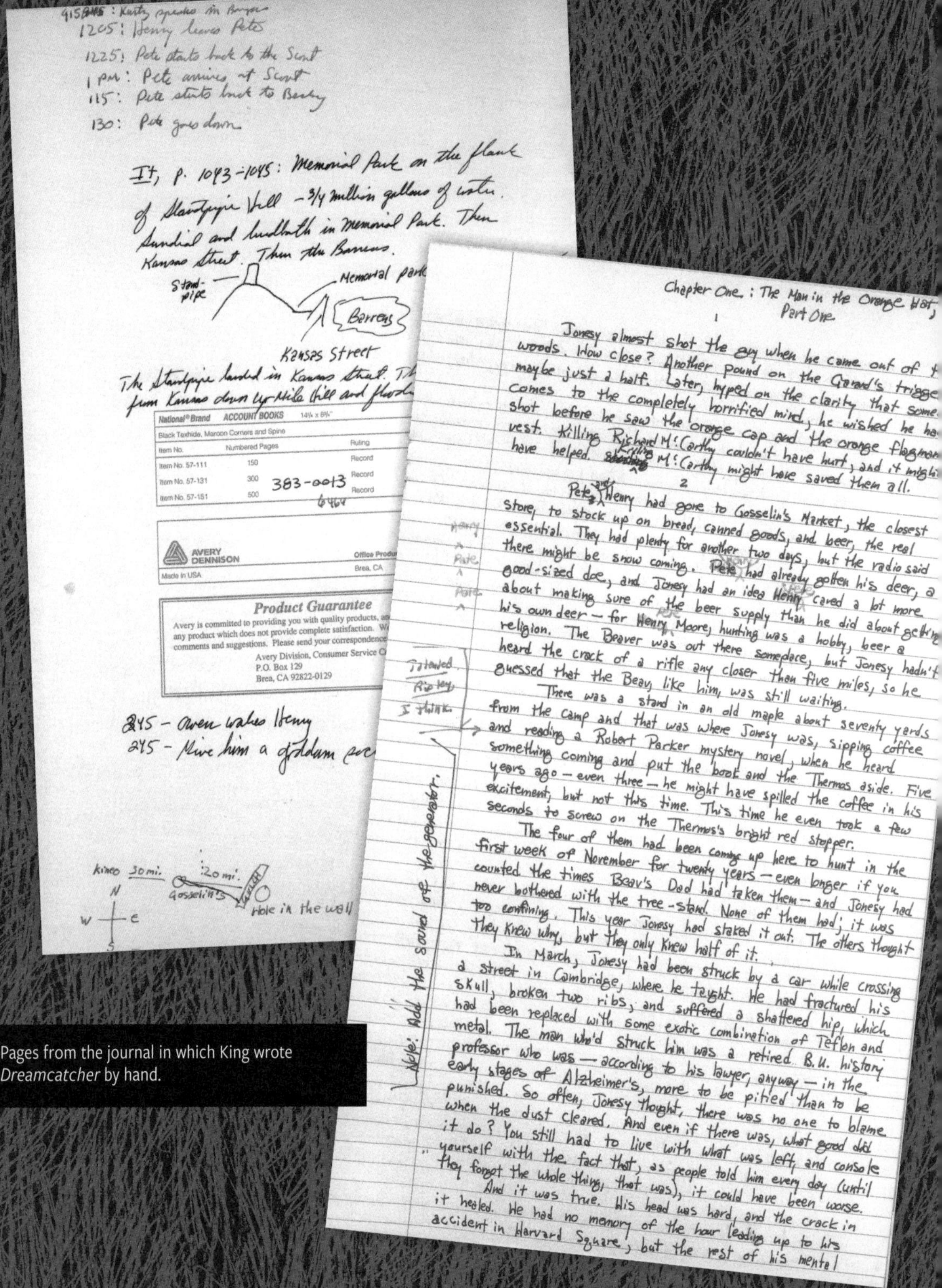

Pages from the journal in which King wrote *Dreamcatcher* by hand.

9158X5: Kirsty speaks in Bangor
1205: Henry leaves Pete
1225: Pete starts back to the Scout
1 PM: Pete arrives at Scout
115: Pete starts back to Beaver
130: Pete goes down

It, p. 1043-1045: Memorial Park on the flank of Standpipe Hill – 3/4 million gallons of water. Sundial and birdbath in memorial Park. Then Kansas Street. Then the Barrens.

Stand-pipe ——— Memorial park
Barrens

Kansas Street

The Standpipe landed in Kansas Street. Th... from Kansas down Up-Mile Hill and flood...

National® Brand ACCOUNT BOOKS 14¼ x 8⅞"
Black Texhide, Maroon Corners and Spine

Item No.	Numbered Pages	Ruling
Item No. 57-111	150	Record
Item No. 57-131	300	Record
Item No. 57-151	500	Record

383-0043
0464

AVERY DENNISON
Made in USA
Office Produ...
Brea, CA

Product Guarantee
Avery is committed to providing you with quality products, a... any product which does not provide complete satisfaction. W... comments and suggestions. Please send your correspondence...

Avery Division, Consumer Service C...
P.O. Box 129
Brea, CA 92822-0129

245 - Owen wakes Henry
245 - Give him a goddam soc...

Kites 30mi. 20mi.
Gosselin's
Hole in the well
W—E N S

Chapter One: The Man in the Orange Hat,
Part One.

1

Jonesy almost shot the guy when he came out of t... woods. How close? Another pound on the Garand's trigge... maybe just a half. Later, hyped on the clarity that some... comes to the completely horrified mind, he wished he ha... shot before he saw the orange cap and the orange flagm... vest. Killing Richard McCarthy couldn't have hurt, and it migh... have helped. ~~Shooting~~ ~~Killing~~ McCarthy might have saved them all.

2

Pete & Henry had gone to Gosselin's Market, the closest store, to stock up on bread, canned goods, and beer, the real essential. They had plenty for another two days, but the radio said there might be snow coming. Pete had already gotten his deer, a good-sized doe, and Jonesy had an idea Henry cared a lot more about making sure of the beer supply than he did about getting his own deer — for Henry Moore, hunting was a hobby, beer a religion. The Beaver was out there someplace, but Jonesy hadn't heard the crack of a rifle any closer than five miles, so he guessed that the Beav, like him, was still waiting.

There was a stand in an old maple about seventy yards from the camp and that was where Jonesy was, sipping coffee and reading a Robert Parker mystery novel, when he heard something coming and put the book and the Thermos aside. Five years ago — even three — he might have spilled the coffee in his excitement, but not this time. This time he even took a few seconds to screw on the Thermos's bright red stopper.

The four of them had been coming up here to hunt in the first week of November for twenty years — even longer if you counted the times Beav's Dad had taken them — and Jonesy had never bothered with the tree-stand. None of them had; it was too confining. This year Jonesy had staked it out. The others thought they knew why, but they only knew half of it.

In March, Jonesy had been struck by a car while crossing a street in Cambridge, where he taught. He had fractured his skull, broken two ribs, and suffered a shattered hip, which had been replaced with some exotic combination of Teflon and metal. The man who'd struck him was — according to his lawyer, anyway — in the early stages of Alzheimer's, a retired B.U. history professor who was, more to be pitied than to be punished. So often, Jonesy thought, there was no one to blame when the dust cleared. And even if there was, what good did it do? You still had to live with what was left, and console yourself with the fact that, as people told him every day (until they forgot the whole thing, that was), it could have been worse.

And it was true. His head was hard, and the crack in it healed. He had no memory of the hour leading up to his accident in Harvard Square, but the rest of his mental

[margin notes, right page:]
Henry ^
Pete ^
Pete ^
Pete ^

Totaled
Rip Torn
I think

Little: Add the sound of the generator.

At the end of *On Writing*, Stephen includes a list of nearly a hundred novels he considers the best he'd read in the previous few years. "A good many of these might show you some new ways of doing your work. Even if they don't, they're apt to entertain you," he concludes.[171]

DREAMCATCHER (2001)

The first story Stephen published after his accident was "Riding the Bullet." It is probably no coincidence Stephen chose to name the rollercoaster featured in the story after one of the dogs owned by Bryan Smith, the driver of the van that struck him. His first postaccident novel, and his first full-length novel in three years, was *Dreamcatcher*. Stephen wrote the first draft entirely by hand in hardcover ledgers between November 1999 and May 2000.

As with most of his books, the novel began with a single image. "When I went to bed at night, I would lie there and I'd think of this guy on a hunter stand, in a tree. . . . And I thought, here's this guy, it's starting to snow, he wants to get his deer because it's hunting season, and here comes this thing he thinks is a deer, but it's a person . . . . That's all I had. . . . I started to write it long hand, not expecting much, hoping it might help with the pain a bit. And suddenly I had this huge, huge book, a thousand pages long. All out of that one situation."[172]

One of the four main characters in the novel, Jonesy, was struck by a car and has barely recovered enough to join his friends on their annual camping trip in western Maine. The sense of "before and after" is part of Jonesy's reality. The character thinks of the version of himself from before the accident as "the whole Jonesy." He is a man in constant discomfort and pain, reflecting Stephen's condition at the time he was working on the novel.

"I was in a lot of physical discomfort during those six and a half months, and the book took me away," he writes in the author note at the end of the book. "To write the first draft of such a long book by hand put me in touch with the language as I haven't been for years," Stephen reflects. "I even wrote one night (during a power outage) by candlelight. One rarely finds such opportunities in the twenty-first century, and they are to be savored."[173]

Tabitha refused to refer to the book by his original title, *Cancer*. "She considered it both ugly and an invitation to bad luck and trouble. Eventually I came around to her way of thinking, and she no longer refers to it as 'that book' or 'the one about the shit-weasels,'" he writes in the afterword.[174]

The book also gave Stephen the chance to explore a cultural taboo. "I'd never really read a story about something terrible happening revolving around bathroom functions," he told *Time* magazine. "And I wanted to do that because it just occurred to me that so much of the really terrible news we get in our lives, we get in the bathroom. . . . Half of really scaring people is getting them in a place that's undefended. Nobody's as defenseless as they are in the bathroom, with their pants down."[175]

Years later, Stephen admitted he didn't like the book very much. "I was pretty stoned when I wrote it, because of the Oxy, and that's [a] book that shows the drugs at work," he told *Rolling Stone* magazine.[176]

EVERYTHING'S EVENTUAL (2002)
"Autopsy Room Four," "The Man in the Black Suit," "All That You Love Will Be Carried Away," "The Death of Jack Hamilton," "In the Deathroom," "The Little Sisters of Eluria," "Everything's Eventual," "L.T.'s Theory of Pets," "The Road Virus Heads North," "Lunch at the Gotham Café," "That Feeling, You Can Only Say What It Is in French," "1408," "Riding the Bullet," "Luckey Quarter"

As Stephen promised in *Nightmares & Dreamscapes*, *Everything's Eventual* contains only stories published after that earlier collection, dating from 1994 to 2001. Rather than agonize over the order in which the thirteen stories should appear in the collection or presenting them chronologically, Stephen came up with an interesting idea. He assigned the stories numbers and shuffled the spades from a deck of card (plus a joker), arranging the stories in the corresponding order after he dealt them. "And it actually created a very nice balance between the literary stories and the all-out screamers," he says.[177]

FROM A BUICK 8 (2002)
During a road trip from Florida to Maine in early 1999, Stephen stopped at a gas station in Pennsylvania. While stretching his legs behind the station, he slipped, tumbled down a slope, and nearly ended up in a swollen stream at the bottom.

AN HONOR TO BE NOMINATED

Critical opinion toward Stephen King has changed over the years. In the 1980s, *Time* dismissed his writing ability by calling him the "Master of Post-Literate Prose." Stephen famously called himself "the literary equivalent of a Big Mac and fries." However, the establishment started taking him more seriously after his work appeared in literary magazines such as the *New Yorker* and the *Paris Review*.

In addition to awards for individual works, Stephen has been given Lifetime Achievement Awards by the World Horror Convention, the Horror Writers Association, the International Horror Guild, the World Fantasy Convention, Mystery Writers of America, and Canadian Booksellers Association (he was the first non-Canadian to receive this honor), among others.

In 2003 he received the Medal for Distinguished Contribution to American Letters from the National Book Foundation, and in 2014 President Barack Obama presented him with the National Medal of Arts from the National Endowment for the Arts. In 2016, the Library of Congress acknowledged him for a Lifetime of Work Promoting Literacy, and in 2018 he received the PEN America Literary Service Award.

His awards haven't always been flattering. He was also nominated for the 1986 Golden Raspberry Award for Worst Director (*Maximum Overdrive*), but he lost to Prince (*Under the Cherry Moon*).

President Barack Obama presents author Stephen King with the 2014 National Medal of Arts at The White House on September 10, 2015 in Washington, DC.

STEPHEN KING

From A Buick 8

A Novel

The incident made him wonder how long it would have taken for someone to realize he was missing and to find him—or his body—in the gulley. In the book's afterword, he writes, "This little incident happened around ten in the morning. By afternoon I was in New York. And by then I had the story you've just read pretty much set in my mind."[178] King says his inspiration for the book's setting came from K.C. Constantine's police procedural novels featuring small-town police chief Mario Balzic.

Two months later, in the middle of June, he finished the first draft of *From a Buick 8*, a novel inspired by that incident. Instead of conducting research beforehand, Stephen prefers to complete a draft and then determine what is necessary. He says, "When I'm writing a book, my attitude is: don't confuse me with facts."[179] In this case, a return to Pennsylvania was in order, to visit with troopers and state police to learn the details of their daily lives. But it would be fourteen months before Stephen would get a chance to make that research trip. A week or so after he finished the first draft, Stephen was struck by a van and almost killed.

In the opening pages of *From a Buick 8*, State Trooper Curtis Wilcox is struck and killed by a drunk driver who is leaning over to extract a beer from a cooler on the floor next to him. When the book was published three years later, that incident seemed like it had been inspired by Stephen's experience. However, it was a case of life imitating art, for Stephen had written that scene months earlier. "The coincidence of having written a book filled with grisly vehicular mishaps shortly before suffering my own has not been lost on me, but I've tried not to make too much of it. . . . I changed nothing in the course of my story to reflect what happened to me; most of what I wanted was there in the completed draft. The imagination is a powerful tool."[180]

That doesn't mean he didn't make changes. "The book was done in a first draft, but I wasn't satisfied with it. After the accident, I was able to sit down with a fresh eye." Publication of the novel was postponed because it didn't seem appropriate so close to his own accident.[181]

From a Buick 8 was the last book in his contract with Scribner. Although the final three *Dark Tower* books had yet to be published, Stephen implied in an interview he might retire. "I'm done," he told the *Los Angeles Times*. "Done writing books. . . . I've said the things that I have to say, that are new and fresh and interesting to people. Then you have a choice. You can either continue to go on, or say I left when I was still on top of my game."[182]

He was less adamant in subsequent interviews, but when *Time* asked him directly, he responded, "I can't imagine retiring from writing. What I can imagine doing is retiring from publishing. If I wrote something that I thought was worth publishing, I would publish it. But in terms of publishing stuff on a yearly basis the way I have been, I think those days are pretty much over."[183]

FAITHFUL (2004)

It could have become a horror story when Stephen and fellow writer Stewart O'Nan decided to write a book based on the 2004 Red Sox baseball season from spring training through the postseason. The Red Sox had long been considered a "cursed" team, getting close to the championship several times without a World Series since 1918. Expectations were high in 2004 for the team after a disappointing end to their previous season, but there was no guarantee of a positive outcome.

In late 2003, O'Nan's agent suggested he write a book about the Red Sox. Stephen and O'Nan had been emailing each other about the team throughout 2003, but it was too late to cover that season. O'Nan said he would only do it if he could convince Stephen to collaborate. Stephen agreed to contribute, although his initial idea was that O'Nan would do most of the writing and he would chime in from time to time. O'Nan and King attended some games together and each kept a diary about the team's performance during the season. They had two ground rules—they would not go back and change anything they'd already written, and they would not try to get inside the clubhouse to talk to the players, preferring to present their impressions purely from the perspective of fans.

As the season progressed, Stephen's participation grew. When the Red Sox fell to ten games back in June, slipping out of wild card contention for a while, Stephen emailed O'Nan, "Oh, this is maddening. Why why why did I ever let you talk me into this?"[184]

King signs copies of *Faithful*, co-authored with Stewart O'Nan, at the offices of publisher Simon & Schuster in December 2004.

The Red Sox ultimately won a wild card spot in the playoffs and swept the Angels in their first postseason matchup. Then they had to face their longtime rivals, the New York Yankees, and immediately lost the first three games in the best of seven series. No team had ever come back from such a deficit in major league history. The irony of having relief pitcher Tom Gordon playing for the Yankees—and playing well—was not lost on Stephen. To everyone's surprise, the Red Sox prevailed, advancing to the World Series finals. In a scene that would seem unbelievable in a novel, they won the World Series during a lunar eclipse and a blood-red moon. *Faithful: Two Diehard Boston Red Sox Fans Chronicle the Historic 2004 Season* didn't end up being a horror story after all.

THE COLORADO KID (2005)

Hard Case Crime was launched in 2004 with a mission to publish a mix of lost pulp masterpieces from acclaimed crime writers of the past and new novels from the next generation of hardboiled authors, all with covers painted in the pulp style. Aware of Stephen's love for the genre, the founder asked if he would be willing to write a blurb for the line of books. Stephen decided he'd rather endorse them by supplying a book instead.

The Colorado Kid takes places on an island off the Maine coast, where an unidentified man was found dead years earlier. The mystery intrigues a pair of local newspapermen, but after a year of investigation all they succeed in doing is identifying the man, the Colorado Kid. The more they dig, the stranger the case becomes. It seems like an impossible crime committed under baffling circumstances. Stephen says, "I think it has some of those old-fashioned kick-ass story-telling virtues. It ought to; this is where I started out, and I'm pleased to be back."[185]

CELL (2006)

Once upon a time, Stephen was leaving a New York hotel to grab a hot drink. "A lady under the canopy was on her cell phone and the doorman was getting someone a cab. I thought, what if she got this message on her cell phone that she could not deny and she had to attack everyone she saw—and she started with the doorman."[186] This was the image that inspired his novel *Cell.*

Stephen said, "I carried the basic idea for *Cell,* and the characters, in my head for five years before breaking the logjam that was keeping me from writing it (geography—when I stopped being fixated on New York and decided to start in Boston, I was fine)."[187]

If Richard Bachman could have foreseen the cell phone era before his untimely death, *Cell* might have had his name printed on the cover. In *The Stand,* people on the side of good banded together to help everyone survive in the new order. In

STEPHEN KING
SPORTS FAN, SPORTSWRITER

Stephen's affinity for baseball is no secret. He is one of the Boston Red Sox's biggest fans, often seen in the stands at their games, usually with a book in hand to read between innings. For many years, he shaved off his beard at the beginning of spring training and put his razor away after the World Series.

Stephen went to his first Red Sox game at Fenway in 1959 and claims he went at least once a year for the next ten years and never saw the Red Sox lose.[188] He devoted one of his King's Garbage Truck columns in the *Maine Campus* to the 1969 World Series.

His characters are usually Red Sox fans—as early as in the 1975 short story "The Lawnmower Man." In the *Dark Tower* series, both Father Callahan and John Cullum ask Eddie Dean if the Red Sox ever win the World Series in their futures. These are men contemplating the fate of the universe, but they still find time to talk baseball.

Stephen and Tabitha donated the money for the construction of Shawn T. Mansfield Stadium, a top-notch baseball facility built to NCAA specifications in Bangor. The stadium, which opened in 1992 and is known locally as the Field of Screams, is visible from the Kings' Bangor home.

Stephen used a Red Sox pitcher as the title character in *The Girl Who Loved Tom Gordon* and revisited baseball a few years later in *Blockade Billy*. "People have asked me for years when I was going to write a baseball story. Ask no more; this is it," he said. "I love old-school baseball, and I also love the way people who've spent a lifetime in the game talk about the game. I tried to combine those things in a story of suspense."[189]

In 1999, he contributed an essay to Major League Baseball's magazine about the Boston Red Sox's relentless pursuit of the World Series. That same year, as he lay in a hospital after being hit by a van, he asked for details of a Red Sox win, which doctors took as a positive sign for his recovery.

When Stephen threw the opening pitch at a game at Fenway in 2004 (his pitch appeared in the baseball movie *Fever Pitch*), the *Boston Globe* blamed Stephen for jinxing the Red Sox when they lost that night, ending a ten-game winning streak.

He told the *Boston Globe*, "I've often thought that I would like to write a story or even a novel where some columnist finds this old guy who's never seen the Red Sox lose. He's been to a lot of games and they find out that when they bring this guy into the park, they always win, so they prop him up and get to the World Series and the guy has a couple of strokes and a heart attack and they're still bringing him in. Of course, the kicker is, he dies before the seventh game."[190]

Cell, it's basically every survivor for himself. People eye each other with mistrust, expressing "a rather shabby lack of interest in anyone other than themselves."[191]

Stephen wrote *Cell* while working on revisions to *Lisey's Story*. He wanted to publish *Lisey's Story* first, but his publisher wanted to put *Cell* on a fast track. That meant he had to work on the rewrite immediately after completing the first draft instead of letting the book rest before revising it for publication.[192] The winner of a charity auction got to have a character in the book named after her brother.

Although Stephen professed to hate cell phones at the time, his publisher devised a marketing plan to send a text message to 100,000 cell-phone users saying, "The next call you take may be your last." It had a link to a site where people could purchase cell-phone wallpapers and ringtones featuring Stephen's voice. Stephen tried to convince his publisher to record a ringtone that had him repeating, "Don't answer it," but Scribner rejected that idea.[193]

LISEY'S STORY (2006)

In November 2003, Stephen was awarded the Medal for Distinguished Contribution to American Letters from the National Book Foundation. He wasn't the first popular author to win the award, but something about him winning riled the literary establishment.

His acceptance speech was primarily a love letter to his wife, Tabitha. What the audience didn't know was that the award meant so much to Stephen he literally risked his life to accept the medal and deliver his speech. The lung that had been punctured by one of his ribs in 1999 hadn't healed properly, leading to a serious case of pneumonia. His doctors had advised against attending the banquet—they wanted him to go straight to the hospital. Instead, Stephen put on a brave face and masked his discomfort. The next day he entered the hospital, where he stayed for nearly two months. It was the second time the van accident almost killed him.

While he was in the hospital, Tabitha decided to redecorate his home studio. He remembers, "When I came back, she said, 'I wouldn't go in there; it's disturbing.' So of course I went in there, and it was disturbing. . . . [T]he furniture had been pulled out because my wife was getting it reupholstered, and the rugs had been rolled up. I thought, This is what this place is going to look like after I die. . . . When I thought of my wife cleaning out my papers, a light went on. *Lisey's Story* bloomed from that."[194]

OPPOSITE: Stephen King attends a signing of his novel *Lisey's Story* at Borders on Oxford street in London on November 7, 2006.

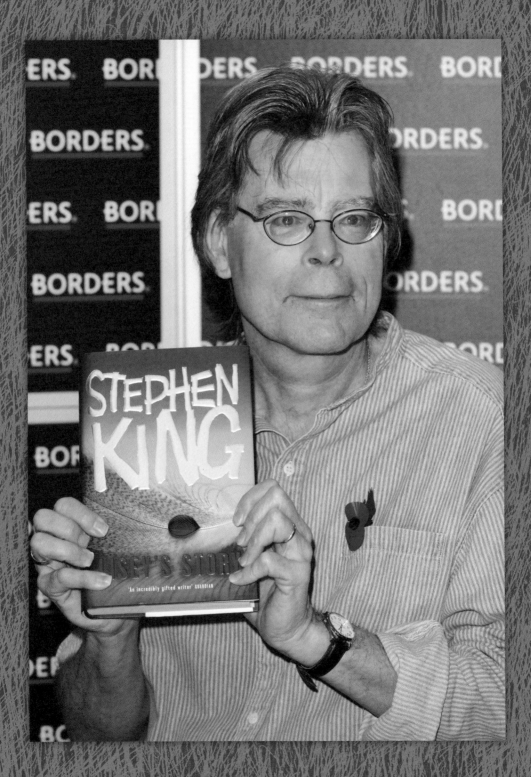

It took Stephen a while to recover from his prolonged hospitalization, but he started on the novel right away. He originally intended for *Lisey's Story* to be a funny book about the spouse of a famous writer. "I wanted to show that his wife got completely ignored, but was the person responsible for all his success," he said. "Then this guy Dooley came on the scene and wanted the writer's manuscripts and the story took a different direction. It got more serious."[195]

Bag of Bones and *Lisey's Story* form bookends—in the former, the writer has to learn how to survive in the aftermath of his wife's death, while in the latter, the opposite is true. However, Lisey Landon is still living as if her husband Scott were

BLOOM ON KING/KING ON BLOOM

The late Harold Bloom, self-proclaimed defender of the literary canon, was not Stephen King's number one fan. In his introduction to a volume he edited containing essays analyzing King's works, he concludes, "I cannot locate any aesthetic dignity in King's writing. . . . King will be remembered as a sociological phenomenon, an image of the death of the Literate Reader." He later called King a writer of "penny dreadfuls," declared the decision to award King the medal for Distinguished Contribution to American Letters "another low in the shocking process of dumbing down our cultural life. . . . What he is is an immensely inadequate writer, on a sentence-by-sentence, paragraph-by-paragraph, book-by-book basis."

King responded, "Harold Bloom has never been very interested in popular culture, and he has no real grasp of popular culture, popular writing, or the places where what we call pop culture crosses what you would call higher culture. . . . What I would really like to do is see Harold Bloom given an injection of sodium pentothal so that he had to tell the truth and say, 'Now, Harold, how much Stephen King have you actually read?' And I think that the answer would be probably less than one whole book. My guess is he's dipped a few times, and you come to the table with certain prejudices, and naturally you're going to see those prejudices fulfilled."

with her. Two years after his death, Scott's office looks like he could walk in at any moment, sit at his desk, and start writing again. His voice is alive in her head and his untouched office is a metaphor for her suppressed grief. She's finally decided it's time to pack up certain things, figure out what to do with all of his books and papers, and move on.

Stephen isn't interested in writing about death itself. He says, "If there's an afterlife it's so hypothetical that it almost doesn't bear thinking about as a writer. What does interest me is what happens to love in the wake of death and how it lasts."[196]

Stephen creates such an intimate depiction of a long, successful marriage, Tabitha worried readers would assume he was writing about their life. He took pains to point out the differences during his publicity tour for the book.

Instead of using his regular editor, Stephen handed the first-draft manuscript over to Nan Graham, the editor-in-chief at Scribner. He is very aware that many people believe bestselling authors like him refuse to be edited. He dismissed that notion, saying, "I would be happy to submit sample pages from my first-draft manuscript, complete with Nan's notes. I had first-year French essays that came back cleaner."[197]

The novel spans about a week of contemporary time and a quarter of a century of history. Scott and Lisey's love story plays out in reverse. Lisey has forgotten some details of her marriage and there were facts about her husband's past she never knew.

Once she rediscovers all the things she's forgotten and learns the truth about her husband's childhood, she can get past her grief. Like the Kings, the Landons started out poor, which strengthened their relationship in the early years. It was them against the world. Because of Scott's tortured past, he refuses to have children—it's the one deal-breaker Lisey must accept if she wants a life with him. It's the only way he knows that will break his family's cycle of violence. As Scott's career took off, he became a celebrity and Lisey fell into his shadow, in public at least. In private, she was the stable ground on which their marriage was built, helping to keep Scott's inherited madness in check.

Scott has an enormous fan base that includes people who want to do him harm, like the guy who shoots him during a groundbreaking ceremony for a university library. As usual, Lisey's role in saving her husband's life that day went unheralded.

Stephen and Tabitha King at the 54th Annual National Book Awards Ceremony and Benefit Dinner in Manhattan on November 19, 2003. King's acceptance speech was in large part a love letter to his wife.

The book revisits Stephen's belief that reality is thin. Boo'ya Moon, the alternate reality where Scott goes when he is injured, is his "myth pool," the source of his literary inspiration. Stephen said once in an interview, "Imagination is a wonderful thing, but it's also a terrible thing. . . . It's sweet in the daytime and awful at night."[198]

Stephen also explores the concept of an author's literacy legacy. Academics and fans would love to get their hands on any unpublished manuscripts Scott left behind. The most ardent collector, a professor from Scott's alma mater, sends a dangerous fan to convince Lisey to release Scott's archives to him.

All of these challenges are part of what makes this Lisey's story; she steps out of the shadow of her husband's fame and their now-absent relationship to become a strong woman who can face the seemingly relentless forces that have aligned against her.

Lisey's Story is Stephen's most personal novel, a mature reflection on his long and successful marriage, his equally long and spectacularly successful writing career, and his thoughts on what might happen after he's gone. It's a book that could only have been written by someone who has lived a full life and is now shifting his focus to encompass the clearing at the end of the path.

BLAZE (2007)

Stephen wrote *Blaze* in late 1972–73, "during the six-month period when the first draft of *Carrie* was sitting in a desk drawer, mellowing."[199] Some of the pages were typed on the reverse sides of milk-bills, he recalls. He called the book a literary imitation of Steinbeck's *Of Mice and Men*.[200] The original typescript was produced using Tabitha's Olivetti typewriter, which she sometimes accused him of marrying her for.

"I thought it was great while I was writing it, and crap when I read it over."[201] He revisited the novel in the early eighties and decided his original judgment had been correct. The manuscript was relegated to his archives for the next three decades. After *The Colorado Kid* was published, his thoughts returned to *Blaze*. His assistant found the original 173-page manuscript and a 106-page partial rewrite in the Fogler Library at the University of Maine.

Stephen reread it and found it was better than he remembered. "I . . . determined to strip all the sentiment I could from the writing itself, wanted the finished book to be as stark as an empty house without even a rug on the floor."[202] In some interviews, he kept up the pretense of Richard Bachman being someone else. "That wasn't my book. That was Richard Bachman's. So, it's just a posthumous novel and I fixed it up for the poor fella . . ."[203]

JUST AFTER SUNSET (2008)

"Willa," "The Gingerbread Girl," "Harvey's Dream," "Rest Stop," "Stationary Bike," "The Things They Left Behind," "Graduation Afternoon," "N," "The Cat from Hell," "*The New York Times* at Special Bargain Rates," "Mute," "Ayana," "A Very Tight Place"

In the introduction to his fourth collection, Stephen writes about how his approach to writing short stories has changed over the years. In the early days, he says, "I wrote them fast and hard, rarely looking back after the second rewrite, and it never crossed my mind to wonder where they were coming from. . . I was flying entirely by the seat of my pants."[204]

THE PHILANTHROPISTS

The Kings are well known in Maine for philanthropy, though their efforts often reach beyond the borders of their home state. Many school and town libraries have been the beneficiaries of grants, and several major development projects in Bangor have been funded in large part by the Kings, including the so-called "Field of Screams" baseball field (Mansfield Park), a swimming complex, hospital wings, and the Bangor Public Library.

The Stephen and Tabitha King Foundation is a private nonprofit organization that supports community initiatives. The Barking Foundation provides grants and scholarships for postsecondary education for Maine residents based on merit and financial need. The Haven Foundation, which was the recipient of the royalties from *Blaze*, provides support for people in the performing arts who are unable to work and have no health insurance. These foundations are occasionally cited as being among the most efficient celebrity charitable organizations.

His short story output had declined over the years, and he grew concerned he was forgetting how to write them. When he was asked to guest edit *Best American Short Stories* in 2006, he agreed immediately, believing that by reading a lot of short stories written by other authors he might be able to "recapture some of the effortlessness that had been slipping away."

There are thirteen stories in *Just After Sunset*, all but one written between 2003 and 2008. "I got excited all over again, and I started writing stories again in the old way. I had hoped for that, but had hardly dared believe it would happen," he writes.

DUMA KEY (2008)

Although Stephen is a long-time resident of Maine, he and his wife started living in Florida for the winter in 1998. "I was walking my dog in our driveway and a chunk of ice dropped off the mailbox, which just missed him. That's when we asked ourselves, 'Why are we still here in the winter?' So we decided to start coming down here."[205]

After nearly a decade of living in the Sunshine State, Stephen finally felt he knew Florida's Gulf Coast well enough to write about it. "You have to know where the roads go and what the names of the plants are," he says.[206]

Stephen was on a walk at his winter home in Florida in 2003 when he saw a sign that said, "Caution: Children." He imagined "two dead girls holding hands like paper dolls." The image persisted and although he didn't use it, "that image got me started."[207] He began work on *Duma Key* in February 2006 and finished the first draft in October, revising it simultaneously with his work on *Blaze*.

Duma Key features a character recovering from a catastrophic accident in which he was permanently maimed. Edgar Freemantle suffers from phantom pains in a lost limb, but he gained something in return: the power to change reality through his paintings.

"I'd heard how creativity, how make-believe, can help the body heal from physical injuries," he said. "I also got interested in psychic phenomena connected to phantom limbs."[208] "Edgar's injuries were worse than mine. I didn't lose an arm, I didn't lose my wife, but like him, my memory was affected. I know a little about pain and suffering and what happens when the painkillers lose their efficacy, when your body gets used to them," he said in an interview. [209]

"If *Desperation* is a book that's full of pain and unhappiness, *Duma Key* is a book where there actually is hope, because I was feeling in a more hopeful place. I was feeling a lot better by the time that I wrote *Duma Key*, and I think it shows in the book."[210]

Duma Key book review illustration by Jim Atherton for the Fort Worth Star-Telegram.

UNDER THE DOME (2009)

Sometimes an idea is too big for a writer to tackle when it first occurs to him. It may be beyond his abilities. The story might require extensive research that a young man who has a family and a full-time teaching job can't afford. The science required to develop an idea may go beyond his expertise and he may not have anyone available to assist him. Or the idea might simply need time to grow.

Stephen does not keep an idea notebook. He has said on numerous occasions he thinks they're the best way to immortalize bad ideas. A good idea will stick around, he believes.

He first had the idea for *Under the Dome* when he was teaching high school in the 1970s. He wrote several dozen pages and then put them aside, ultimately losing the manuscript. In November 2006, Stephen decided to give it another try. He remembered the opening scene in which a woodchuck gets cut in half when a dome materializes around a Maine town, and he rewrote it from memory. When he read that section at an event at the Library of Congress the following year, he said, "I waited twenty-five years to write it, because I tried this once before when I was a lot

King holds a glass dome to promote CBS's miniseries *Under the Dome*.

younger and the project was just too big for me, and I let it go, I let it slide, but it was a terrific idea that never entirely left my mind. . . . Every now and then it would say 'Write me,' so finally I did."[211]

A mysterious, invisible dome descends over Chester's Mill, Maine, one sunny mid-October Saturday morning, preventing its inhabitants from leaving town and anyone or anything from entering. People can communicate through it, but it is unmovable and, apparently, unbreakable. There is limited air exchange (an important factor for the town's long-term survival), and a jet of water directed at the outside produces only a fine mist inside. The electric lines are down but—thanks to the prevalence of generators in western Maine—cell phones, cable TV, and the internet all work.

THE CANNIBALS

In the 1980s, Stephen wrote the first 450 pages of a novel called *The Cannibals* that explores how characters behave when they're cut off from society. For a long time, he believed the manuscript had been lost. However, shortly before *Under the Dome* was published, it turned up in his office, battered, and with some pages missing, but mostly complete. He posted the first 120 pages on his website.

The Cannibals is set in an apartment building in a city west of Philadelphia. Its residents are cordial to each other but aren't on friendly terms. One morning, people find they are unable to leave for work. The outer doors simply refuse to budge. The outside light is an unusual hue. The nearby freeway has no traffic and the cars in the parking lot look so hyper-real that they seem like mirages. Phone calls go through, but the person on the other end can't hear the caller. The building's windows can't be broken. Panic and confusion build.

"It is all about these people who are trapped in an apartment building. Worst thing I could think of. And I thought, wouldn't it be funny if they all ended up eating each other? It's very, very bizarre. . . . And who knows whether it will be published or not?"[212]

King promotes *Under The Dome* at a Walmart in Dundalk, Maryland on November 11, 2009.

The world is aware of the town's plight. Attempts to breach it are broadcast live on television. People speculate it was created by an extraterrestrial intelligence or a rogue state.

Stephen is less interested in the origins of the dome or what the world thinks about it than in exploring what happens to the residents trapped inside. They worry about how long their food and propane will last, how the dome will affect their weather, and when the air will no longer be safe to breathe. People seize the opportunity for personal benefit. Tempers flare and old grudges are rekindled.

The book's villain is Big Jim Rennie, a used-car dealer and member of the town council. He has been embezzling money and running an illicit drug operation. As long as the dome remains in place, his illegal activities won't be discovered. He seizes power to maintain control of the situation. Opposing him is a group led by Dale "Barbie" Barbara, an Iraq war veteran who is returned to active duty to provide intelligence to his former commanding officer about the situation in Chester's Mill.

Though the book drew early comparisons to *The Stand*, there are fundamental differences between the two. *The Stand* was a chess game, while *Under the Dome* is a rapid-paced game of checkers. The story is geographically limited and the timespan much briefer. Both books explore the nature of good and evil, but in *The Stand* these concepts were taken to an absolute level. God is not a character in *Under the Dome*. The sincerest "religious" character is a minister who doesn't believe in God anymore. The town leaders are not Evil—merely evil.

ADAPTATIONS

Compared to the previous decade, the period between 2000 and 2009 was relatively quiet on the adaptation front. Few of the big-screen releases have had a lasting impact. *Dreamcatcher* was a critical flop, although *Hearts in Atlantis* and *1408* were considered moderately successful. On the small screen, *The Dead Zone* ran for six seasons and the anthology series *Nightmares & Dreamscapes* adapted eight of Stephen's short stories.

The trend of remaking earlier movies and series emerged with a second miniseries based on *'Salem's Lot* and a remake of *Carrie*. And, yes, there were two more *Children of the Corn* movies.

See Appendix II for an extensive list of adaptations.

EASTER EGGS

Easter eggs, those sly little inside jokes creators plant in their films, software, or video games as a nod to people familiar with the genre or subject, have been part of Stephen King's adaptations since the early days.

Some adaptations embrace Easter eggs while others ignore them altogether, preferring to keep the audience immersed in the current story. The TV series *Haven*, loosely adapted from *The Colorado Kid*, had at least one—if not several—references to something from the Stephen King Universe in every episode. The 2021 version of *The Stand* was packed full of Easter eggs,[213] including a sly cameo by Stephen, who appears on a bus stop poster for a senior-citizen complex called Hemingford Home (the hometown of one of the book's characters).

Stephen has created his own basket of Easter eggs in his novels and stories. Some are in the form of crossover references to his other works, but others are simply things that show up regularly. There's a Ford Pinto in *Billy Summers*, for example, which may remind readers of *Cujo*. Billy mentions that his mother worked in a commercial laundry, running the "mangle," which Stephen's Constant Readers will recognize. And how many characters wear blue chambray shirts?

A lot.

THE STEPHEN KING UNIVERSE

Stephen's novels are interconnected, with characters from one story appearing in another, and events from earlier novels being referenced in subsequent books. Cataloging all these connections is beyond the scope of this book—it would require a massive volume to do so. One such book, *The Complete Stephen King Universe*, took three authors to compile and is well over 500 pages—and that's just for the first two decades of Stephen's career. One fan has created a poster-size map outlining all the major connections in Stephen's work. It resembles one of those conspiracy theory string charts from a thriller movie.

There are two kinds of connections in Stephen's books. The first are the kind where characters acknowledge they're living in a world where Stephen King is a living, breathing person, and not their creator (more on that later). This happens for the first time in *The Dead Zone*, where someone says, "He set it on fire by his mind, just like in that book *Carrie*."

In the *Dark Tower* series, Nigel the android has read *The Dead Zone* and Eddie Dean is familiar with the Steadicam scenes from *The Shining* even though he had no idea who Stephen King was. He was soon to find out. Thanks to a magic door that sent him to Maine in the 1970s, Eddie got to meet the man who was writing the story that was his life.

It's only natural, too, that people who live in Castle Rock or Derry would know about the incidents that took place there in the past. Some of these events were sufficiently significant that they would be known across the state, so it's not surprising when someone mentions that rabid dog that killed the sheriff, or the homicidal crossing guard.

What is surprising is when a character from one book suddenly pops up in another, seemingly unrelated book. This happens most frequently in *The Dark Tower* series, where Father Callahan (*'Salem's Lot*), Patrick Danville (*Insomnia*), Ted Brautigan (*Hearts in Atlantis*), and "Dinky" Earnshaw (*Everything's Eventual*) all end up in Roland Deschain's Mid-World, as do two boys from *The Eyes of the Dragon*. There are many other examples of these character crossovers.

Sometimes the connections are inevitable. When Billy Summers ends up in the mountains above Sidewinder, Colorado, it is not a surprise that he should hear about the supposedly haunted Overlook Hotel that burned to the ground there years before (*The Shining*).

There are also subtle connections, like when Ralph Roberts discovers a sneaker belonging to Gage Creed (*Pet Sematary*) in *Insomnia*. Song lyrics quoted in *Duma Key* are attributed to R. Tozier and W. Denbrough, two characters from *It*.

Finally, there's the mystical number nineteen, which started appearing in Stephen's work in *The Dark Tower* series because that was the date of his near-fatal accident. From that point on, the number is either used directly (as a street address or highway designation, for example) or indirectly (the number of letters in a character's name, the sum of the digits in a combination). Stephen's fans have also found the number in older works, which only goes to show that, as Stephen says, everything is nineteen.

6

King of Crime
(2010 and Beyond)

A few major themes dominate Stephen's work after 2010. First, he reached a point in his career where he felt ready to tackle concepts he had postponed or dismissed because he didn't feel he could do them justice when he first had the ideas. He also revisited a character from one of his most famous novels to find out what had happened to him in the decades since Stephen had first explored a traumatic incident in the young boy's life.

Finally, he wrote frequently and at length in a genre that he has long enjoyed as a reader but rarely explored as a writer. Stephen's fondness for the crime genre revealed itself in several books published in the 2010s and beyond, although he often added his own particular twist to the genre.

FULL DARK, NO STARS (2010)
1922, Big Driver, Fair Extension, A Good Marriage

The stories in Stephen's third novella collection are as dark as the title suggests. These are violent stories that show people in terrible situations—some of their own creation and others not. Stephen does not shy away from the violence. He describes it in gruesome detail.

The first story, *1922*, was inspired by the nonfiction book *Wisconsin Death Trip* by Michael Lesy. It is in the form of a confessional by a man who murdered his wife because she wanted him to sell their farm and move into the city. He forced their son to become a coconspirator in the crime, leading to the family's ultimate doom.

Stephen got the idea for *Big Driver* when he saw a woman, whose car had a flat tire, talking to a truck driver at a rest stop. *Fair Extension* was inspired by a street vendor who operated near the Bangor airport. When Stephen read an article about a serial killer, he wondered what the spouse of a serial killer might know about her husband's activities, which led him to write *A Good Marriage*.

At least two of the stories have no supernatural elements, and there are no happy endings. "You may have found [these stories] hard to read in places," Stephen writes in the afterword. "If so, be assured that I found them equally hard to write in places . . . if you're going into a very dark place . . . then you should take a bright light, and shine it on everything."[214]

11/22/63 (2011)

In 1971, when Stephen was teaching high school, some of his fellow teachers were gathered in the lounge reflecting on the anniversary of the John F. Kennedy assassination. Someone asked, "What would the world be like if Kennedy had lived?" They debated the series of coincidences that had to come together for Lee Harvey Oswald to be in the right place at the right time to kill the president.

Inspired by this conversation, Stephen began a novel called *Split Track* about a man who goes back in time to stop the assassination. He wrote about fourteen single-spaced pages before abandoning it. Research was a major stumbling block. There were so many real people who would have to be characters, he couldn't afford to travel to do research, and he was overwhelmed by having to use details of the past in a way that would seem real. He also thought the pain of the assassination was too fresh in people's minds in 1971.

The idea persisted, though, and forty years later *11/22/63* was published. In the book, people travel through a portal located in the storeroom of Al Templeton's diner in Lisbon Falls, Maine. They always emerge in that town at 11:58 a.m. on September 9, 1958. No matter how long a visitor stays there, when he returns to the present only two minutes have elapsed. If anyone goes through the "rabbit hole" again, alterations to the timeline made on the previous journey are undone. Every trip is like the first time—or so Al believes.

School teacher Jake Epping teaches an adult GED program to make more money. (GED stands for General Educational Development, and people in the program achieve a high school diploma equivalency.) Otherwise, he lives a quiet life, alone except for a cat. He has few friends, so he has little to lose when Al nominates him for a mission the cook can no longer attempt himself.

Of all the events that abruptly changed the course of humanity—the terrorist attacks in 2001, the failed Hitler assassination, or the murder of Archduke Ferdinand that started World War I, for example—only one is within reach of Al's time portal: the Kennedy assassination. Al has already tried to stop it once, but during the five years he had to pass while waiting for 1963, he came down with cancer. However, he did manage to amass a great deal of research and resources that will make Jake's task easier.

Once Jake confirms that the changes he makes in the past do have an impact on the present, he sets out on his mission. In theory, he could simply track Oswald down and kill him right away, but he's not convinced Oswald acted alone.

Besides, Oswald won't return from Russia for several years. Jake also has to come up with a plan that won't see him spending the rest of his life in prison—in the past— for murder.

Everything he does sends ripples of change down the timeline, so he has to watch the way he speaks and avoid making references to things that don't yet exist. However, the past is resistant to major changes, throwing hurdles in Jake's path whenever he attempts to do something that will have serious implications for the future.

Jake discovers he doesn't like Dallas very much. It's a city with a dark veil, menacing in much the same way Derry was. He moves to Jodie, a small town well

OPPOSITE: Full dust jacket of Scribner's hardcover edition of *11/22/63.*; RIGHT: Jake Epping (James Franco) and Bill Turcotte (George MacKay) listen in on Lee Harvey Oswald to try to prevent the assassination of John F. Kennedy in the Hulu miniseries *11.22.63.*

outside the city, and starts a new life as a teacher. He wasn't looking for love, but that's what he finds with Sadie Dunhill. While *11/22/63* is a time-travel novel on the surface, at its heart it is a love story. The fact that Jake has to hide his mission from Sadie, while learning to negotiate the early 1960s, doesn't make his life any easier.

Stephen hasn't always been a huge fan of research. He likes to make things up and then fill in the details later. However, the amount of research he undertook while writing this novel is impressive. He recounts some of it in the afterword, including details of his week-long trip to Dallas with a researcher friend. The two were granted a private tour of the Book Depository, including the "sniper's nest" corner that is blocked off from the public. They also visited Oswald's apartment building and paid a resident to let them look inside.

The book's biggest tragedy is Jake's awareness that he can't stay in 1963 if his mission succeeds. He has to return to his own time to confirm Al's theory the world

THE POP OF KING

Between July 2003 and January 2013, Stephen wrote a column called "The Pop of King" for *Entertainment Weekly* magazine. In it he discussed pop culture, sometimes covering more controversial topics like politics.

He wrote over 125 essays in this nearly ten-year span, often using the column to draw attention to authors, books, musicians, movies, or TV programs he thought were at risk of being overlooked. He wrote about adaptations of his work, bad TV ads, his love of *Breaking Bad*, *The Wire*, and *Lost*, writing book blurbs and what movie blurbs really mean, movie snacks, pet peeves, the Oscars, audiobooks, the arrival of e-book readers, and many other things.

This wasn't Stephen's first gig addressing pop culture. From early 1969 until his graduation from the University of Maine, he wrote a weekly column called "King's Garbage Truck" for the *Maine Campus*. Back then, he wrote about TV game shows, movies, The Beatles, baseball, the pressures of being a student, and campus and global politics.

The Texas School Book Depository facing Dealey Plaza in Dallas, Texas. Lee Harvey Oswald shot President John F. Kennedy from a window on the sixth floor of this building.

will be a better place if Kennedy hadn't been killed. Stephen discussed the possible outcomes with Tabitha (a history major) and with historian Doris Kearns Goodwin, one of Lyndon Johnson's aides, and her husband, Dick Goodwin, who was part of the Kennedy team. Their insights into Kennedy's effectiveness as a leader and what might have happened if he had survived influenced Stephen in deciding what Jake would discover when he goes home. Although Stephen is sometimes faulted for the way he ends his epic novels, he pulls off a thoroughly unexpected, satisfying, and touching coup with the finale of *11/22/63*.

DOCTOR SLEEP (2013)

At public appearances over the years, people often asked Stephen what happened to Danny Torrance from *The Shining*. Stephen usually joked Danny married Charlie McGee from *Firestarter* and they had the most amazing kids. However, privately he wondered where Danny went after his terrible experience.

In 2009, while onstage at an event in Toronto, Stephen said that, although he ended *The Shining* on a positive note, the Overlook was bound to have left young Danny with a lifetime's worth of emotional scars. He had a title for a possible sequel—*Doctor Sleep*—but he thought the time for writing it had passed. Encouraged by the response to a reader poll on his website, though, he decided to tackle the novel.

While preparing to write *Doctor Sleep*, Stephen reread *The Shining*. He was now more than twice the age he was when he wrote it. "I've learned some new tricks since then," he said in an interview. He was concerned about people's reaction to his following up on an older work. "The whole sequel idea is really dangerous. I think

Ewan McGregor as adult Dan Torrance in Mike Flanagan's film adaptation of *Doctor Sleep*.

people have a tendency to approach them with a raised eyebrow like, 'Hmm, if this guy is going back to where he was thirty or thirty-five years ago he must be low on ideas.'" He stressed that this book is not a sequel to the film, at the end of which the Overlook is still standing and Dick Halloran is dead.[215]

The book's prologue deals with Danny and Wendy several years after they escaped the Overlook. They're now living in Florida and are in frequent contact with Dick Halloran. Danny is having disturbing visions, so Dick visits to give him some tools to deal with the ghosts of the hotel that won't leave him alone.

Later in *Doctor Sleep*, Danny, now a recovering alcoholic, takes a job in a hospice in New Hampshire. His special powers allow him to ease the pain of the dying in their final days and hours. His "shine" also puts him in touch with a powerful twelve-year-old girl named Abra Stone. Abra becomes a target of the True Knot, a group of vampire-like characters led by a woman who calls herself Rose the Hat. She is a source of the psychic energy they need to live longer.

At George Mason University, Stephen read a section about the True Knot. Instead of sucking blood, they absorb psychic energy from special people like Danny Torrance while they are being tortured. They see Abra as an almost endless supply of the psychic energy they require to extend their lives. Members of the True Knot have to

keep on the move, because they are prone to changing their appearances overnight, jumping forward or back as much as twenty years at a time, which would attract unwanted attention. Stephen wondered how they traveled without being detected. His answer came from his experiences driving between Florida and Maine each year. He told an audience that, for him, the scariest things at rest areas and on highways are the RVs. Stephen conjures the image of retired senior citizens in gaudy tourist apparel who monopolize rest stops with their convoys of oversized, bumper-sticker-covered Winnebagos. They form long, slow queues at fast-food restaurants located near full-service exits from the interstate, waffling over their orders.

Stephen believed that critics had recently been speculating he was finally getting away from writing horror. "They won't know what hit them when they read *Doctor Sleep*," he said. "It's a . . . scary book." He reiterated this on his website, saying, "If you're looking for a return to . . . keep-the-lights-on horror, get ready. And don't say you weren't warned."[216]

JOYLAND (2013) AND LATER (2021)

Despite his link to horror, Stephen also has a lifelong relationship with the mystery genre. As a child, he often bought paperback crime novels when he went shopping with his mother, and he loved Agatha Christie's mysteries. However, he couldn't figure out how to construct detailed puzzles like hers. "I was never built to be the sort of writer who plots things," he said. "I usually take a situation and go from there."[217]

Many of his early short stories featured gangsters and hitmen. While *The Colorado Kid* flirted with the unknowable, *Joyland*, Stephen's second paperback novel with Hard Case Crime, is a whodunit seasoned with supernatural elements. It is about a college student who goes to work at a North Carolina amusement park in 1973, where he confronts the legacy of a vicious murder and the fate of a dying child. The book's editor says it is about growing up and growing old, and about those who don't get to do either because death comes for them before their time.[218]

For his third Hard Case Crime book, however, Stephen goes all in. There are mystery elements to *Later*, but as narrator young James "Jamie" Conklin reminds readers on several occasions, this is a horror story. Jamie can see and talk to dead people, but only for a short period after they die. His mother, a literary agent, realizes early on what her son can do, and knows that people will exploit it for their own benefit. It's ironic, then, that it is Jamie's mother who first falls prey to this temptation.

"I wanted to write about a literary agent because I never had," Stephen says. "One client that this agent has who is worth big bucks dies suddenly. What's she going to do about it? What if she has a kid who can see dead people and they have to answer any question that he asked? And I thought, 'I got a story.'"[219] After deciding Jamie's mother needed a companion, he thought, "'Cop,' and the cop is dirty and everything fell into place."[220]

MR. MERCEDES (2014), FINDERS KEEPERS (2015), AND END OF WATCH (2016)

There is a similar progression in the three books in the *Mercedes* trilogy. The first, *Mr. Mercedes*, is a straight crime novel. *Finders Keepers* contains subtle hints of the unexplainable, and *End of Watch* is undeniably supernatural.

Mr. Mercedes was inspired by a news story about a woman who drove her car into a crowd of people during an altercation with another woman, killing two and injuring several others. He knew he wanted to write about it, but he didn't yet know how. After rolling the idea around in his mind for nearly a year, he came up with a story about a retired homicide detective who receives a letter from a man who deliberately

committed a similar crime, which came to be known as the City Center Massacre. The killer's taunting message inspires the retired cop to look into a case that might have otherwise gone unsolved. Stephen thought this idea would turn into a twelve-page story, but he ended up with a 500-page manuscript instead.

Even before the first book came out, Stephen had decided he wasn't done with this fictional world. There would be three books, but the unifying element would not be the detective or the villain, as is often the case with series, but rather the City Center Massacre. Everyone killed that day had a story and the survivors had an aftermath.

Finders Keepers is, in part, about books, writers, and writing. Why are some authors remembered while others are forgotten? The book's villain, Morris Bellamy, has the same belief as did Annie Wilkes in *Misery*: The author of his favorite books owes him something, especially when a particular story takes a turn he doesn't like. He's angry that author John Rothstein has disrespected his most famous creation, Jimmy Gold, and he'll do anything to get his hands on Rothstein's unpublished manuscripts.

End of Watch completes the saga and adds a supernatural twist to the series.

Although Stephen has demonstrated an ease with the crime genre, he finds those books harder to write than his other novels. Even so, in 2007, the Mystery Writers of America bestowed upon him their highest accolade: the Grand Master Award, which represents the pinnacle of achievement in the mystery field.

REVIVAL (2014)

Stephen has had one of the core ideas for *Revival* since he was a kid. That was when he first read "The Great God Pan" by Arthur Machen, a story that stayed with him throughout his life. He describes it as "a terrifying story about the world that might exist beyond this one"[221] and said he wanted to write about bringing somebody back

OPPOSITE: King is presented the Grand Master Award at the Mystery Writers Of America's Edgar Awards ceremony, honoring the best in mystery fiction, nonfiction, television and film on April 26, 2007. ABOVE: King signs copies of *Revival* on November 15, 2014 in Austin, Texas.

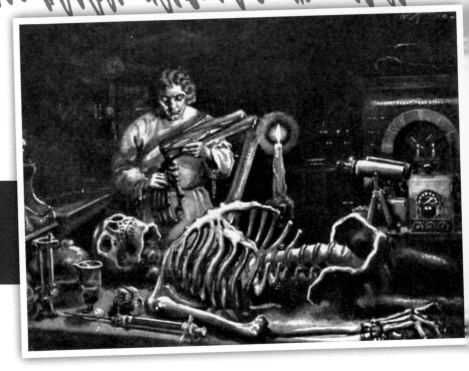

Illustration from a 1922 American edition of *Frankenstein* by Mary Shelley, which was an inspiration for King's novel *Revival*.

to life someday. He was also influenced by *Frankenstein*, wanting to write about a mad scientist who was a real human being rather than a cartoon character.

He started working on the novel in Maine in April 2013, after he finished *Mr. Mercedes*, and completed it in December at his house in Florida. *Revival* also presented him with the opportunity to write about rock and roll. Stephen says he's not very good at guitar, but he loves to play.

The main character's descent into addiction was also something Stephen was familiar with, although he says his craft is now fueled by gallons of tea rather than drugs and alcohol. The book is autobiographical in other aspects. Stephen made use of his religious upbringing. "I . . . wanted to talk a little bit about what is beyond death," he said, "because the Reverend has lost his wife and his son, and he's very curious about whether or not there's some sort of afterlife."[222]

Finally, Stephen's goal was to write a full-on supernatural horror story, something he hadn't done in a long time. Falling back on a familiar baseball analogy, he confessed he had slowed down a bit in the way baseball pitchers often do when they age. "I'm old, but I'm not dead, so I can still wind up and fire."[223] He called *Revival* a "fastball," showing he could still bring it.

THE BAZAAR OF BAD DREAMS (2015)

"Mile 81," "Premium Harmony," "Batman and Robin Have an Altercation," "The Dune," "Bad Little Kid," "A Death," "The Bone Church," "Morality," "Afterlife," "Ur," "Herman Wouk is Still Alive," "Under the Weather," "Blockade Billy," "Mister Yummy," "Tommy," "The Little Green God of Agony," "That Bus is Another World," "Obits," "Drunken Fireworks," "Summer Thunder"

The Bazaar of Bad Dreams contains eighteen stories and two poems. The already-published stories are from 2009–2015, and several formerly appeared as e-books or audiobooks. "Bad Little Kid," was previously only available as an e-book in French and German, a thank-you gift Stephen offered to his overseas fans after a successful tour of those countries. "Ur" was a Kindle-only story and "Mile 81" was another e-book original. "Drunken Fireworks" is a hilarious story initially released only on audio.

GWENDY'S BUTTON BOX (2017), ELEVATION (2018), AND GWENDY'S FINAL TASK (2022)

In July 2016, Stephen had an idea about a modern Pandora. "She was the curious little girl, you'll remember, who got a magic box and when her damned curiosity (the curse of the human race) caused her to open it, all the evils of the world flew out. What would happen, I wondered, if a modern little girl got such a box, given to her not by Zeus but by a mysterious stranger. . . ."[224]

Stephen started writing the story of twelve-year-old Gwendy Peterson, who was presented with a strange box covered with colored buttons for safekeeping. However, the story ran out of gas, and he turned to something else, although he thought about Gwendy from time to time.

In January 2017, a conversation with his friend Richard Chizmar inspired Stephen to send him the incomplete manuscript, telling Richard to finish it if he was so inspired. Richard was captivated by the story of a young girl's strange experience in Castle Rock, and the two authors completed the novella, editing each other's work.

Working on the story renewed Stephen's interest in Castle Rock, a town he hadn't thought about in a while. This interest led to the novella *Elevation*, which is also set in Castle Rock. Stephen said *Elevation* is "almost like a sequel to Gwendy. Sometimes you seed the ground, and you get a little fertilizer, and things turn out."[225]

COLLABORATIONS

Although writing is normally a one-person job, Stephen has occasionally collaborated with other authors. Although he cowrote very short stories with his sons when they were young, Stephen's first published collaboration was the fantasy novel *The Talisman*, with Peter Straub. To short-circuit the guessing game about who wrote what, the authors came up with an interesting solution. "I tried to write like him, he tried to write like me, and we met somewhere in the middle,"[226] Stephen said. The fact that the authors both revised each other after the book was finished helped blur the lines to the point where Stephen and Straub have admitted they aren't sure who wrote what parts anymore. They reunited for the sequel, *Black House*, and had discussed plans for a third book featuring Jack Sawyer. However, Straub died in 2022, so if there is a third book, Stephen will write it by himself.

Stephen has written two published short stories with his son Joe Hill. He had this to say about working with his elder son: "His style and my style, we don't write the same but we're in harmony with one another. The thing kind of flows naturally."[227]

Ghost Brothers of Darkland County is a different kind of collaboration—one in which Stephen developed a story outline presented to him by Grammy Award-winning musician John Mellencamp. Together they created a Southern Gothic musical that tells the story of two brothers haunted by their past.

Stephen's sole non-fiction collaboration, *Faithful*, written with Stewart O'Nan, led to another collaboration between the two authors: "A Face in the Crowd," a baseball-themed short story.

Stephen teamed up with son Owen for the fantasy novel *Sleeping Beauties*. "To be asked by Owen to collaborate on a book was the greatest thing in the world," Stephen told *Entertainment Weekly*. "You see these signs that say Smith & Son's hardware or stuff. So, sons do follow in their father's footsteps. But in a specialized area of one of the arts? It was very gratifying to me."[228] Stephen also cowrote two novels with Richard Chizmar.

Stephen summed up his thoughts about working with other people this way: "At the end of the day, what makes a good collaboration is respect for the person that you're collaborating with."[229]

"I wouldn't want to do it all the time, mostly I like having the playhouse to myself."[230]

A couple of years later, Richard Chizmar approached Stephen with an idea for a new story about Gwendy. Stephen was intrigued, but he was working on *End of Watch*, so he gave Richard the green light to write what would become the novel *Gwendy's Magic Feather* on his own. Scribner felt there were some unique marketing opportunities available if there could be a third book, completing a trilogy. Stephen came up with a new idea for a Gwendy adventure, so the two authors went back to work on *Gwendy's Final Task*, which takes Gwendy on an out-of-this-world adventure.

SLEEPING BEAUTIES (2017)

Pitching story ideas is a common occurrence in the King household. Stephen's youngest son, Owen, came up with one that sounded like something his father would write: a global epidemic where all the women in the world go to sleep and any of them that are disturbed in their cocoons become violent. Stephen could immediately see the ramifications of this concept but told Owen he should write it. Eventually they agreed to work on it together.

Sleeping Beauties was originally conceived as a limited TV series. The Kings wrote a pilot and a follow-up episode, but Owen felt hemmed in by the format. He wanted to explore the characters beyond what one-hour episodes allowed. For the next two years they tossed the novel back and forth, ending up with a long first draft. "I'd have it for three or four weeks and he'd have it for maybe three or four weeks or maybe a little bit longer," Stephen said.[231]

THE OUTSIDER (2018)

Stephen has explored the concept of the outsider numerous times in previous works, including such entities as Pennywise from *It* and the creature that possesses the ghost of Sara Tidwell in *Bag of Bones*. In a discussion of fear, he says, "What are we afraid of, as humans? Chaos. The outsider."[232]

In *The Outsider*, he explores the idea in the framework of the crime novel. "*The Outsider* is about how we react when we are faced with the inexplicable," Stephen says.[233] The novel involves a seemingly impossible situation. Only someone who has investigated a crime with supernatural implications can begin to understand what's going on. That person is Holly Gibney from the *Mr. Mercedes* trilogy, who is now a private detective specializing in inexplicable crimes.

THE INSTITUTE (2019)

For this book, Stephen imagined a schoolhouse filled with kids with supernatural abilities. He saw *The Institute* as a resistance story rather than a horror novel. "I wanted to write about how weak people can be strong," Stephen told the *New York Times*. "We're each on our own island, and at the same time sometimes we can yell to each other and get together, and there is that sense of community and empathy. . . . I love that in stories."[234]

At first, Stephen thought about using The Shop, the government agency from *Firestarter*, as the villain of the piece. Ultimately, he discarded that idea, using "privately funded zealots" instead.

IF IT BLEEDS (2020)
Mr. Harrigan's Phone, The Life of Chuck, If It Bleeds, Rat

When talking about *Mr. Harrigan's Phone*, the first novella in the collection, Stephen recalls seeing a horror movie when he was a kid about a man so afraid of being buried alive that he had a phone installed in his crypt. "Years later, after a close friend died unexpectedly, I called his cell phone just to hear his voice one more time. Instead of comforting me, it gave me the creeps. I never did it again."[235]

The second story is one of the most intriguing things Stephen has ever written. *The Life of Chuck* is told in three parts, in reverse. In the author note, Stephen says he has no idea where the idea for the story came from. "What I can say is that I've always felt that each one of us . . . contains the whole world."[236]

The title story was inspired by nightly news coverage. For the past decade, Stephen noticed the same reporter covering disasters. "I thought to myself, wouldn't it be weird if a guy like that set off these tragedies?"[237]

The final story, *Rat*, deals with a character who catches influenza after shaking hands with someone sick and failing to wash his hands afterward. Sensing people needed something to read during the pandemic lockdown, Scribner released the collection a few weeks earlier than originally planned.

BILLY SUMMERS (2021)

With *Billy Summers*, Stephen returns to the realm of non-supernatural crime thrillers. The novel was inspired by an image of a man in a basement apartment watching feet go by on the sidewalk outside the building. Stephen wondered why the man was there. "After playing with that for a while, I thought of this same guy in an office building, on the fifth or sixth floor of a building near a courthouse. What's he doing there? Well, he's going to shoot somebody. He's going to shoot a bad guy."[238]

Stephen originally set the novel in 2020. Then the pandemic happened. He had a couple of characters he needed to sideline for a while. His initial solution was to send them on a cruise, but that industry had shut down. Since the book also involves a lot of cross-country travel, he decided to move it back to 2019 rather than try to figure out a way to handle the coronavirus problem.

Although *Billy Summers* is not a supernatural novel, it has a connection to the ruined hotel from *The Shining*. "It was a conscious nod to longtime readers. . . . It's like a tip-of-the-hat to the genre."[239]

The book also explores the act of writing. "There are books that I've written where writing is seen as sort of a toxic thing, and there are only a couple, *Misery* is one, and *Billy Summers* is another, where it talks about writing as salvation. You don't have to be a professional writer to know that that's the case sometimes. It's a doorway into your own feelings and your own view of the world. So that's a good thing."[240]

FAIRY TALE (2022)

In an interview, Stephen explained the origins of the story: "What could you write that would make you happy? As if my imagination had been waiting for the question to be asked, I saw a vast deserted city—deserted but alive. I saw the empty streets, the haunted buildings. . . . I saw a huge, sprawling palace with glass towers so high their tips pierced the clouds. Those images released the story I wanted to tell."[241]

The novel is a return to epic fantasy on the scale of *The Talisman* and *The Dark Tower*. A seventeen-year-old boy named Charlie Reade befriends an elderly man who leaves him a legacy: a portal to another world in the shed behind his house. In that alternate universe, a war is being waged that may destroy both worlds.

HOLLY (2023)

When Stephen read a headline about a "sweet old couple" who had buried bodies in their backyard, he knew he had an idea for a novel. He also decided to write a book set during the pandemic and he had the perfect character to use in such a story: Holly Gibney, who was supposed to be only a minor character in *Mr. Mercedes*. Stephen says she stole both that book and his heart. Holly is a hypochondriac, which makes her very cautious during the pandemic, observing all the recommended safety precautions. Her mother died from COVID-19 and Holly had to attend her funeral over Zoom.

Stephen says Holly will also appear in a novel called *We Think Not*, although she will not be the main character.

YOU LIKE IT DARKER (2024)

"Two Talented Bastids," "The Fifth Step," "Willie the Weirdo," "Danny Coughlin's Bad Dream," "Finn," "On Slide Inn Road," "Red Screen," "The Turbulence Expert," "Laurie," "Rattlesnakes," "The Dreamers," "The Answer Man"

This is a different kind of collection for Stephen, combining five new long stories with a number of recently published short stories. One of the new stories, "Rattlesnakes," is a sequel to *Cujo*, featuring Vic Trenton, now a widower, who goes to a Florida coastal island similar to the one in *Duma Key* to sort through his grief.

WE THINK NOT (TBA)

Stephen returns to the Finders Keepers agency and Holly Gibney, although she's not the main character. "Jerome [Robinson] is involved with this one particularly because in a lot of the early books, Jerome's job . . . has to do with finding lost dogs or kidnapped dogs. So I had a chance to do something in this book with that, and I'm really delighted to see him involved in the book. He's a cool character," he told *Rolling Stone*. [242]

ADAPTATIONS

The 2010s launched a second Golden Age for Stephen adaptations. The advent of a variety of streaming platforms meant that the types of stories found in Stephen's work could be adapted for the small screen without censorship. Several high-quality,

King on the set of the first season
of the TV series *Under the Dome*.

big-box-office movies inspired other directors and producers to adapt Stephen's work. When the trailer for *It: Chapter One* set a record, with nearly 200 million views within the first twenty-four hours,[243] expectations for the film were cautiously optimistic. The movie, when released, set numerous records for the amount of revenue generated by an R-rated horror movie, bringing in over $700 million worldwide against a $35-million budget. Suddenly, everyone wanted to make Stephen King movies again.

On smaller screens, there were several feature-length adaptations. The series based on *Under the Dome* limped along for three seasons before being canceled. However, the series *Haven*, inspired by *The Colorado Kid*, ran for six seasons, and *Castle Rock*, inspired by Stephen's fictional town and some of his characters and incidents, aired for two seasons.

See Appendix II for an extensive list of adaptations.

OTHER ADAPTATIONS

When we talk about adaptations, we usually refer to movies or miniseries or TV episodes, but Stephen's work has been adapted in several other ways. There are the graphic novel adaptations, mentioned elsewhere, but there are also plays, operas, podcasts, games, and even songs.

The most famous—some would say infamous—theatrical adaptation of Stephen is a 1988 musical based on *Carrie*, reputed to be the biggest flop in Broadway history. After previews, it only ran for five regular performances.

Misery also made its way to Broadway (without music), with Bruce Willis and Laurie Metcalf in the leading roles, and there have been plans to produce *The Shining* on Broadway as well.

Over a dozen songs inspired by Stephen's stories have been recorded, including several by Anthrax. Stephen's favorite band The Ramones wrote "Pet Sematary" for the original movie adaptation.

Two of Stephen's works have been adapted as games: *The Mist*, a text adventure game and *The Dark Half*, a point-and-click adventure game.

CONCLUSION

Some people believe it is possible to learn about a writer through a careful reading of his or her work. Others think a writer's work is best understood by knowing the details and circumstances of that person's life. Which way does the mirror point—or does it work in both directions?

The events described in this book can be seen as the bricks that make up the wall that roots his fiction in reality. The previous chapters demonstrate how many of Stephen's books were inspired—at least in part—by what was going on in his life at the time. Though ideas for books can originate anywhere—a personal experience, overheard conversation, a news item, a dream—the stories arising from these ideas that resonate the strongest are the ones that are informed by real life. Stephen establishes a close bond with his readers by incorporating his sharp observations about people and daily life into his stories.

As a result, readers identify with his characters, even those that are caught up in circumstances well beyond human experience. People aren't likely to encounter a ghost, or a vampire, or a possessed car, but if they did, they would probably react in the ways Stephen describes in his books. He believes one of the most important things a writer has to do is tell the truth—even when he's making things up.

What will Stephen's legacy be? He admits he has a vision of how he'd like to be remembered: "You never know what's going to happen. . . . I think any writer would like to be remembered and be somebody who's read, you know, somebody whose work stands the test of time, so to speak. But on the other hand, as a person, I'll be dead, and . . . if there is an afterlife I got an idea that what goes on here is a very minor concern. But you know, I'm built a certain way and the way I'm built is to try and give people pleasure. That's what I do. I want people to read the books and be knocked out and I'd like that to continue even after I stop."[244]

"I've gotten better in some ways, but you lose a little of the urgency. In my 40s, the ideas were like people jamming into a fire door to get out. There were so many ideas, and you couldn't wait to get to the typewriter and the words would pour out. . . . Nowadays, you're almost feeling people are looking over your shoulder and they're apt to be a little more critical. You slow down a little bit. I'm aware I'm getting older."[245] Stephen also expresses some skepticism about his longevity. "I've never fooled myself that I'm going to have much popularity beyond my lifetime."[246]

However, he also admits, "A lot of people my age are forgotten and I've had this late season burst of success. It's very gratifying." He has a theory about why his work has received more positive critical attention in the second half of his career. "I have outlived most of my most virulent critics. It gives me great pleasure to say that. Does that make me a bad person?"[247]

Of course, this isn't the end of the story. Stephen is still writing. Despite his occasional talk about retiring, either from writing or simply from publishing, it doesn't appear he has any plans to slow down. He summed up his thoughts this way: ". . .I'll know when it's time. I'll either collapse at my desk or the ideas will run out—the thing you don't want to do is embarrass yourself. As long as I feel like I'm still doing good work, I can't see myself stopping."[248]

SELECTED BIBLIOGRAPHY

Danse Macabre, Stephen King, Everett House, 1981. In addition to being a compendium of the best in horror movies and novels, it contains "An Annoying Autobiographical Pause," which is among his earliest autobiographical writings.

Stephen King: The Art of Darkness, Douglas E. Winter, New American Library, 1984. This was the first extensive examination of Stephen King and his works. Winter had full access to Stephen, and while limited to the first decade of his publishing career, this book remains one of the best combinations of biography and literary criticism. An updated edition in 1986 includes a discussion of the Bachman books.

Bare Bones: Conversations on Terror with Stephen King, Tim Underwood and Chuck Miller, eds. McGraw-Hill, 1988. The first of two books that reprint interviews that Stephen King granted during the previous decade. Most of these interviews were never widely circulated before their appearance in these volumes.

Feast of Fear: Conversations with Stephen King, Tim Underwood and Chuck Miller, eds. Carroll & Graf, 1992. The second collection of interviews, some dating back as far as 1973.

Secret Windows, Stephen King, Book-of-the-Month Club, 2000. Released as a companion to *On Writing*, this is a collection of essays and book introductions by Stephen, along with a few works of short fiction, including two juvenile stories from *Dave's Rag*, the newspaper his brother published in 1959–1960.

On Writing, Stephen King, Scribner, 2000. A combination of autobiography and advice for writers. In the "C.V." section, Stephen outlines his credentials for the latter, an entertaining and insightful look at his writing career and personal history.

The Complete Stephen King Universe, Stanley Wiater, Christopher Golden, and Hank Wagner, St. Martin's Griffin, 2006. An updated version of their 2001 book, which tracks the connections among all of Stephen's works and the ways in which his plots and characters intertwine.

Haunted Heart: The Life and Times of Stephen King, Lisa Rogak, Thomas Dunne Books, 2009. An unauthorized biography that pieces together events in Stephen's life based on previous writings, extensive research, and new interviews with people who have been associated with Stephen over the years, including the author of this book.

Stephen King: A Literary Companion, Rocky Wood, McFarland & Company, 2011. A two-part companion to Stephen's works. The first part contains essays about his literary legacy. The second section is an encyclopedic list of all characters, settings, and works by Stephen through *Under the Dome*.

Hearts in Suspension, Jim Bishop, ed. University of Maine Press, 2016. In addition to a lengthy autobiographical essay by Stephen called "Five to One, One in Five," the book contains reproductions of four "King's Garbage Truck" columns from his time at the University of Maine, vintage photographs, and reminiscences from some of his college classmates.

APPENDIX I
BOOKS BY STEPHEN KING

Carrie (1974)

'Salem's Lot (1975)

The Shining (1977)

Rage (1977)

Night Shift (1978)

The Stand (1978)

The Long Walk (1979)
   [by Richard Bachman]

The Dead Zone (1979)

Firestarter (1980)

Roadwork (1981)
   [by Richard Bachman]

Danse Macabre (1981)

Cujo (1981)

The Running Man (1982)
   [by Richard Bachman]

The Gunslinger (1982)

Different Seasons (1982)

Christine (1983)

Cycle of the Werewolf (1983)

Pet Sematary (1983)

The Eyes of the Dragon (1984)

The Talisman (1984)
   with Peter Straub

Thinner (1984)
   [by Richard Bachman]

Skeleton Crew (1985)

It (1986)

The Drawing of the Three (1987)

Misery (1987)

The Tommyknockers (1987)

The Dark Half (1989)

*The Stand: The Complete &
   Uncut Edition* (1990)

Four Past Midnight (1990)

The Waste Lands (1991)

Needful Things (1991)

Gerald's Game (1992)

Dolores Claiborne (1992)

*Nightmares &
Dreamscapes* (1993)

Insomnia (1994)

Rose Madder (1995)

The Green Mile (1996)

Desperation (1996)

The Regulators (1996)
   [by Richard Bachman]

Wizard and Glass (1997)

Bag of Bones (1998)

*The Girl Who Loved Tom
   Gordon* (1999)

Hearts in Atlantis (1999)

Storm of the Century (1999)

*On Writing: A Memoir
   of the Craft* (2000)

Dreamcatcher (2001)

Black House (2001)
   with Peter Straub

Everything's Eventual (2002)

From a Buick 8 (2002)

Wolves of the Calla (2003)

Song of Susannah (2004)

The Dark Tower (2004)

Faithful (2004)
   with Stewart O'Nan

The Colorado Kid (2005)

Cell (2006)

Lisey's Story (2006)

Blaze (2007)
   [by Richard Bachman]

Duma Key (2008)

Just After Sunset (2008)

Under the Dome (2009)

Blockade Billy (2010)

Full Dark, No Stars (2010)

11/22/63 (2011)

*The Wind Through
   the Keyhole* (2012)

Joyland (2013)

Doctor Sleep (2013)

Mr. Mercedes (2014)

Revival (2014)

Finders Keepers (2015)

*The Bazaar of
   Bad Dreams* (2015)

End of Watch (2016)

Charlie the Choo-Choo (2016)
   [by Beryl Evans]

Gwendy's Button Box (2017)
   with Richard Chizmar

Sleeping Beauties (2017)
   with Owen King

The Outsider (2018)

Flight or Fright (2018)
   coedited with Bev Vincent

Elevation (2018)

The Institute (2019)

If It Bleeds (2020) *Later* (2021)

Billy Summers (2021)

Gwendy's Final Task (2022)
   with Richard Chizmar

Fairy Tale (2022)

Holly (2023)

You Like It Darker (2024)

We Think Not (TBA)

APPENDIX II
ADAPTATIONS

FILMS (THEATRICAL)

Carrie (1976)

The Shining (1980)

Creepshow (1982)

Cujo (1983)

The Dead Zone (1983)

Christine (1983)

Children of the Corn (1984)

Firestarter (1984)

Cat's Eye (1985)

Silver Bullet (1985)

Maximum Overdrive (1986)

Stand by Me (1986)

Creepshow 2 (1987)

The Running Man (1987)

A Return to Salem's Lot (1987)

Pet Sematary (1989)

Tales from the Darkside (1990)–
  "The Cat from Hell"

Graveyard Shift (1990)

Misery (1990)

Sleepwalkers (1992)

The Lawnmower Man (1992)

Pet Sematary Two (1992)

*Children of the Corn II:
  The Final Sacrifice* (1992)

The Dark Half (1993)

Needful Things (1993)

The Shawshank Redemption (1994)

The Mangler (1995)

Dolores Claiborne (1995)

Thinner (1996)

*Lawnmower Man 2:
  Beyond Cyberspace* (1996)

The Rage: Carrie 2 (1999)

The Night Flier (1997)

Apt Pupil (1998)

The Green Mile (1999)

Hearts in Atlantis (2001)

The Mangler 2 (2002)

Dreamcatcher (2003)

Riding the Bullet (2004)

Secret Window (2004)

Creepshow 3 (2006)

1408 (2007)

The Mist (2007)

Carrie (2013)

A Good Marriage (2014)

The Dark Tower (2017)

It (2017, 2019)

Pet Sematary (2019)

Doctor Sleep (2019)

Children of the Corn (2020)

Firestarter (2022)

The Boogeyman (2023)

The Life of Chuck (2024)

**FILMS (DIRECT TO VIDEO/
MADE FOR TV/STREAMING)**

Sometimes They Come Back (1991)

*Children of the Corn III:
  Urban Harvest* (1995)

*Sometimes They Come Back...
  Again* (1996)

Children of the Corn IV:
  The Gathering (1996)

Trucks (1997)

Sometimes They Come Back...
  for More (1998)

Children of the Corn V:
  Fields of Terror (1998)

Children of the Corn 666:
  Isaac's Return (1999)

Carrie (2002)

Children of the Corn:
  Revelation (2001)

The Diary of Ellen Rimbauer (2003)–
  Prequel to Rose Red

The Mangler Reborn (2005)

Dolan's Cadillac (2009)

Children of the Corn (2009)

Children of the Corn:
  Genesis (2011)

Mercy (2014)–based
  on "Gramma"

Big Driver (2014)

Gerald's Game (2017)

1922 (2017)

Children of the Corn:
  Runaway (2018)

In the Tall Grass (2019)

Cell (2016)

Mr. Harrigan's Phone (2022)

Salem's Lot (2024)

TV EPISODES

"The Word Processor of the Gods"
  (Tales from the Darkside, 1984)

"Gramma"
  (The Twilight Zone, 1986)

"Sorry, Right Number"
  (Tales from the Darkside, 1987)

"The Moving Finger"
  (Monsters, 1991)

"Chattery Teeth"
  (Quicksilver Highway, 1997)

"The Revelations of 'Becka Paulson"
  (The Outer Limits, 1997)

"Gray Matter"
  (Creepshow, 2019)

"Survivor Type"
  (Creepshow, 2020)

TV/STREAMING SERIES/ MINISERIES

Salem's Lot (1979)

It (1990)

Golden Years (1991)

The Tommyknockers (1993)

The Stand (1994)

The Langoliers (1995)

The Shining (1997)

Storm of the Century (1999)

Rose Red (2002)

Firestarter: Rekindled (2002)

The Dead Zone (2002–2007)

Salem's Lot (2004)

Kingdom Hospital (2004)

Nightmares & Dreamscapes (2006)–
  Adapted eight short stories

Desperation (2006)

Haven (2010–2015)–Inspired by
  The Colorado Kid

Bag of Bones (2011)

Under the Dome (2013–2015)

11.22.63 (2016)

The Mist (2017)

Mr. Mercedes (2017–2019)

Castle Rock (2018–2019)

The Outsider (2020)

The Stand (2020–2021)

Lisey's Story (2021)

Chapelwaite (2021)–Inspired
  by "Jerusalem's Lot"

Welcome to Derry (2025)–
  a prequel to *It*

ENDNOTES

1. "On Becoming a Brand Name," *Fear Itself*, Tim Underwood and Chuck Miller, eds. (Underwood-Miller, 1982), 15–42.

2. "Stephen King on Growing Up, Believing in God and Getting Scared," by Terry Gross, *Fresh Air*, May 28, 2013. https://www.npr.org/2013/05/28/184827647/stephen-king-on-growing-up-believing-in-god-and-getting-scared, September 11, 2021.

3. *On Writing* (Scribner, 2000), 28.

4. *The Art of Darkness*, Douglas E. Winter (Plume, 1986), 19.

5. *The Art of Darkness*, Douglas E. Winter (Plume, 1986), 19.

6. *On Writing* (Scribner, 2000), 51.

7. "Guns," (Philtrum Press, 2013), 7.

8. Works→*The Long Walk*→Inspiration, www.stephenking.com, https://stephenking.com/works/novel/long-walk.html, September 25, 2021.

9. *Publishers Weekly*, 2004. https://www.publishersweekly.com/978-1-58767-070-1. September 6, 2021.

10. *The Bazaar of Bad Dreams* (Scribner, 2009), 95.

11. *Stephen King: Man and Artist*, Carroll F. Terrell (Northern Lights, 1991), 33.

12. *Stephen King: Uncollected, Unpublished*, Rocky Wood with David Rawsthorne & Norma Blackburn (Kanrock Publishing, 2006).

13. *On Writing* (Scribner, 2000), 73.

14. "From Textbook to Checkbook," Robert W. Wells, *Milwaukee Journal*, September 15, 1980. Reprinted in *Feast of Fear*. Tim Underwood and Chuck Miller, eds. (Underwood-Miller, 1986), 6-8.

15. Interview with Charles L. Grant, *Monsterland Magazine*, June 1985, 30.

16. *CBS Sunday Morning*, June 13, 2021. https://www.cbsnews.com/news/stephen-king-liseys-story/. September 6, 2021.

17. "On Becoming a Brand Name," *Fear Itself*, Tim Underwood and Chuck Miller, eds. (Underwood-Miller, 1982), 15-42.

18. *Different Seasons* (Viking, 1983), 324.

19. "On Becoming a Brand Name," *Fear Itself*, Tim Underwood and Chuck Miller, eds. (Underwood-Miller, 1982), 15-42.

20. "On The Shining and Other Perpetrations," *Whispers* 17–18, vol. 5, nos. 1–2 (August 1982), 11-16.

21. "On The Shining and Other Perpetrations," *Whispers* 17–18, vol. 5, nos. 1–2 (August 1982), 11-16.

22. "On The Shining and Other Perpetrations," *Whispers* 17–18, vol. 5, nos. 1–2 (August 1982), 11-16.

23. *On Writing* (Scribner, 2000), 95.

24. "The Playboy interview," Eric Norden, *Playboy*, June 1983, 74.

25. Introduction, *The Shining* (Pocket Books, 2001), xv-xviii.

26. Introduction, *The Shining* (Pocket Books, 2001), xv-xviii.

27. "In Their Own Words: An Interview with Stephen King," Paul Janeczko, *English Journal* 69, no. 2 (February 1980), 9–10.

28. *On Writing* (Scribner, 2000), 207.

29. Interview with Michael Kilgore, *Tampa Tribune*, August 31, 1980. Reprinted in *Bare Bones*, Tim Underwood and Chuck Miller, eds. (McGraw-Hill, 1988), 101-111.

30. "King's Shining Returning as a Miniseries," Luaine Lee, *Knight- Ridder/Tribune News Service*, April 20, 1997. http://community.seattletimes.nwsource.com/archive?date=19970420&slug=2534728, September 6, 2021.

31. "On Becoming a Brand Name," *Fear Itself*, Tim Underwood and Chuck Miller, eds. (Underwood-Miller, 1982), 15-42.

32. FAQ, www.stephenking.com, https://stephenking.com/faq/?scroll=why-did-you-write-books-as-richard-bachman-, September 12, 2021.

33. "Why I Was Bachman," *The Bachman Books* (NAL, 1985), v-x.

34. *The Art of Darkness*, Douglas E. Winter, (NAL, 1984), 26.

35. Introduction, *The Shawshank Redemption: The Shooting Script* (Newmarket Press, 1996), ix-xii.

36. "Shine of the Times," Marty Ketchum, Pat Cadigan, and Lewis Shiner. *Shayol* 1, no. 3 (Summer, 1979), 43-46.

37. *Danse Macabre* (Everest House, 1981), 371.

38. *On Writing* (Scribner, 2000), 201.

39. *Danse Macabre* (Everest House, 1981), 371-372.

40. *On Writing* (Scribner, 2000), 203.

41. "Stephen King, The Art of Fiction No. 189," Christopher Lehmann-Haupt and Nathaniel Rich, *The Paris Review*, Issue 178, Fall 2006. https://www.theparisreview.org/interviews/5653/the-art-of-fiction-no-189-stephen-king, September 17, 2021.

42. *The Art of Darkness*, Douglas E. Winter (NAL, 1984), 76.

43. *The Art of Darkness*, Douglas E. Winter (NAL, 1984), 76.

44. Interview with Paul R. Gagne. *Feast of Fear*, Tim Underwood and Chuck Miller, eds. (Carroll & Graf, 1989), 90-108.

45. Interview with Paul R. Gagne. *Feast of Fear*, Tim Underwood and Chuck Miller, eds. (Carroll & Graf, 1989), 90-108.

46. *On Writing* (Scribner, 2000), 192.

47. "Excavating ID Monsters," Stan Nicholls, September 1998. http://www.herebedragons.co.uk/nicholls/interviews.htm, April 5, 2009.

48. *On Writing* (Scribner, 2000), 192.

49. Interview with Michael Kilgore, *Tampa Tribune*, August 31, 1980. Reprinted in *Bare Bones*, Tim Underwood and Chuck Miller, eds. (McGraw-Hill, 1988), 101-111.

50. "On Becoming a Brand Name," *Fear Itself*, Tim Underwood and Chuck Miller, eds. (Underwood Miller, 1982), 15-42.

51. "The Stephen King Interview," David Sherman, *Fangoria: Masters of the Dark* (HarperPrism, 1997), 18.

52. Introduction, "The Sun Dog," *Four Past Midnight* (Viking, 1990), 432.

53. *Faces of Fear*, Douglas E. Winter, (Berkley, 1985), 222.

54. "Stephen King, The Art of Fiction No. 189," Christopher Lehmann-Haupt and Nathaniel Rich, *The Paris Review*, Issue 178, Fall 2006. https://www.theparisreview.org/interviews/5653/the-art-of-fiction-no-189-stephen-king, September 17, 2021.

55. "Digging Up Stories with Stephen King," Wallace Stroby, *Writers On Writing*, September 16, 1991. http://wallacestroby.com/writersonwriting_king.html, September 19, 2021.

56. "Stephen King, The Art of Fiction No. 189," Christopher Lehmann-Haupt and Nathaniel Rich, *The Paris Review*, Issue 178, Fall 2006. https://www.theparisreview.org/interviews/5653/the-art-of-fiction-no-189-stephen-king, September 17, 2021.

57. Peter Straub, interview with Jeff Zaleski, *Publishers Weekly*, August 20, 2001. https://www.publishersweekly.com/pw/by-topic/ authors/interviews/article/28070-pw-talks-with-peter-straub.html September 14, 2021.

58. Afterword, *The Waste Lands* (Donald M. Grant, 1992), 511-512.

59. "Even Stephen King Can't Escape a Quarantine That Feels Like Living in a Stephen King Book," Anthony Brenzican, *Vanity Fair*, April 28, 2020. https://www.vanityfair.com/culture/2020/04/stephen-king-trump-quarantine-the-stand-if-it-bleeds, October 2, 2021.

60. *Different Seasons* (Viking, 1982), 62.

61. "Dear Walden People," *Book Notes*, Waldenbooks, August 1983.

62. "The Once and Future Stephen King," Jill Owens, powells.com, November 22, 2006. https://www.powells.com/post/interviews/the-once-and-future-stephen-king, September 22, 2021.

63. *The Art of Darkness*, Douglas E. Winter, (NAL, 1984), 120.

64. "Banned Books and Other Concerns: The Virginia Beach Lecture," *Secret Windows*, (Book-of-the-Month Club, 2000), 325-330.

65. "Alan D. Williams; appreciation by Stephen King," *Locus*, July 1998.

66. Introduction, *Pet Sematary* (Pocket Books, 2001), ix-xiii.

67. Introduction, *Pet Sematary* (Pocket Books, 2001), ix-xiii.

68. Interview with Mike Farren, *Interview* XVI, no. 2 (1986), 68–70. Reprinted in *Feast of Fear*. Tim Underwood and Chuck Miller, eds. (Underwood-Miller, 1986), 246.

69. Interview with Richard Wolinsky and Lawrence Davison, KPFA- FM, September 8, 1979. From a transcript in *Feast of Fear*, Tim Underwood and Chuck Miller, eds. (Carroll & Graf, 1989), 22-31.

70. "Why I Wrote *The Eyes of the Dragon*," *Castle Rock* Vol 3, No. 2 (February 19876), 4.

71. "Why I Wrote *The Eyes of the Dragon*," *Castle Rock* Vol 3, No. 2 (February 19876), 4.

72. "Jack's Back: Thoughts on the Sequel," *Black House* (Random House, 2001), 639.

73. "The Stephen King interview, uncut and unpublished," Tim Adams, *The Guardian*, September 14, 2000. https://www.theguardian.com/books/2000/sep/14/stephenking.fiction, September 15, 2021.

74. "Stephen King part 2," Hans-Åke Lilja, *Lilja's Library*, January 17, 2007. https://liljas-library.com/cell/showinterview.php?id=35, September 29, 2021.

75. Official website, Works→*Thinner*→Inspiration, https:// stephenking.com/works/novel/thinner.html, November 13, 2021.

76. "The Life and Death of Richard Bachman," Stephen P. Brown, *Kingdom of Fear*, Tim Underwood and Chuck Miller, eds. (Underwood-Miller, 1986), 124.

77. "The Life and Death of Richard Bachman," Stephen P. Brown, *Kingdom of Fear*, Tim Underwood and Chuck Miller, eds. (Underwood-Miller, 1986), 125.

78. "Steven [sic] King Shining Through," Stephen P. Brown, *The Washington Post*, April 9, 1985. https://www.washingtonpost.com/archive/lifestyle/1985/04/09/steven-king-shining-through/eaf662da-e9eb-4aba-9eb9-217826684ab6/, September 20, 2021.

79. "Stephen King Comments on *It*," *Castle Rock* Vol 2, no. 7 (July 1986), 1.

80. Official website, Works→*It*→Inspiration, https://stephenking.com/works/novel/it.html, September 19, 2021.

81. "Stephen King Comments on *It*," *Castle Rock* Vol 2, no. 7 (July 1986), 1.

82. *The Art of Darkness*, Douglas E. Winter (NAL, 1984), 153.

83. Interview with Stephen Schaefer, *Boston Herald*, July 27, 1986. Reprinted in *Feast of Fear*. Tim Underwood and Chuck Miller, eds. (Underwood-Miller, 1986), 192-203.

84. Interview with Stephen Schaefer, *Boston Herald*, July 27, 1986. Reprinted in *Feast of Fear*. Tim Underwood and Chuck Miller, eds. (Underwood-Miller, 1986), 192-203.

85. "The Limits of Fear," Jo Fletcher, Knave 19, no. 5 (1987). Reprinted in *Feast of Fear*. Tim Underwood and Chuck Miller, eds. (Underwood-Miller, 1986), 258-265.

86. "The King of the Macabre at Home," Michael J. Bandler, *Parents* (January 1982). Reprinted in *Feast of Fear*. Tim Underwood and Chuck Miller, eds. (Underwood-Miller, 1986), 221-226.

87. "Stephen King, The Art of Fiction No. 189," Christopher Lehmann-Haupt and Nathaniel Rich, *The Paris Review*, Issue 178, Fall 2006. https://www.theparisreview.org/interviews/5653/the-art-of-fiction-no-189-stephen-king, September 17, 2021.

88. "An Evening with Stephen King," *Secret Windows*, (Book-of-the- Month Club, 2000), 387-401.

89. "A sad face behind the scary mask," Nigel Farndale, *The Sunday Telegraph*, November 25, 2006. https://www.theage.com.au/entertainment/books/a-sad-face-behind-the-scary-mask-20061125-ge3n3y.html, September 15, 2021.

90. "Excavating ID Monsters," Stan Nicholls, September 1998. http://www.herebedragons.co.uk/nicholls/interviews.htm, April 5, 2009.

91. *On Writing* (Scribner, 2000), 166.

92. *Gwendy's Final Task*, Stephen King and Richard Chizmar (Cemetery Dance Publications, 2022) 70.

93. "Stephen King's Scariest Movie Moments," Anthony Timpone, *Fangoria* #238, 2004.

94. *On Writing* (Scribner, 2000), 168.

95. Interview with Ed Gorman, *Mystery Scene* 10, August 1987.

96. "Tabitha King, Co-Miser-ating with Stephen King," *Castle Rock* 3, no. 8 (August 1987), 1.

97. "King Working on Book He Believes Could Be His Best," *Bangor Daily News*, Lynn Flewelling, September 11, 1990. https://web.archive.org/web/20110514104828/https://www.sff.net/people/lynn.flewelling/s.stephen.king.html, April 4, 2024.

98. "Stephen King on His 10 Longest Novels," Gilbert Cruz, *Time*, November 2009. https://entertainment.time.com/2009/11/09/stephen-king-on-his-10-longest-novels/, September 27, 2021.

99. "Stephen King on His 10 Longest Novels," Gilbert Cruz, *Time*, November 2009. https://entertainment.time.com/2009/11/09/stephen-king-on-his-10-longest-novels/, September 27, 2021.

100. *The Art of Darkness*, Douglas E. Winter (Plume, 1986), 170.

101. *Authortalk*, W. B. (Waldenbooks), Volume 1 Number 4, November/December 1989.

102. "Stephen King: The *Rolling Stone* Interview," Andy Greene, *Rolling Stone*, October 31, 2014. https://www.rollingstone.com/culture/culture-features/stephen-king-the-rolling-stone-interview-191529/, September 15, 2021.

103. *Authortalk*, W. B. (Waldenbooks), Volume 1 Number 4, November/December 1989.

104. "Digging Up Stories with Stephen King," Wallace Stroby, *Writers On Writing*, September 16, 1991. https://wallacestroby.com/writersonwriting_king.html, September 19, 2021.

105. *Authortalk*, W. B. (Waldenbooks), Volume 1 Number 4, November/December 1989.

106. *Authortalk*, W. B. (Waldenbooks), Volume 1 Number 4, November/December 1989.

107. "The Importance of Being Bachman," *The Bachman Books* (NAL, 1996), 7.

108. Interview with Janet C. Beaulieu, *Bangor Daily News*, November 1988.

109. "Putting Back the Words," Edwin McDowell, *The New York Times*: Book Notes, January 31, 1990. https://www.nytimes.com/1990/01/31/books/book-notes-059490.html, September 18, 2021.

110. Preface, *The Stand: Uncut and Expanded Edition* (Doubleday, 1990), ix-xii.

111. *Authortalk*, W. B. (Waldenbooks), Volume 1 Number 4, November/December 1989.

112. "King Working on Book He Believes Could Be His Best," *Bangor Daily News*, Lynn Flewelling, September 11, 1990. https:// www.sff.net/people/lynn.flewelling/s.stephen.king.html, March 10, 2011.

113. "A Note on 'The Library Policeman,'" *Four Past Midnight* (Viking, 1990), 483.

114. "A Note on 'The Sun Dog,'" *Four Past Midnight* (Viking, 1990), 737.

115. "Digging Up Stories with Stephen King," Wallace Stroby, *Writers On Writing*, September 16, 1991. http://wallacestroby.com/ writersonwriting_king.html, September 19, 2021.

116. "The Writer Defines Himself: An Interview with Stephen King," Tony Magistrale, *Stephen King: the Second Decade, Danse Macabre to The Dark Half*, (Twayne Publishers, 1992), 17.

117. "Stephen King on His 10 Longest Novels," Gilbert Cruz, *Time*, November 6, 2009. https://entertainment.time.com/2009/11/09/ stephen-king-on-his-10-longest-novels/slide/needful-things-1991/, September 19, 2021.

118. "Bleedful Things," Brad Ashton-Haiste, *Fangoria*, August 1991, 28-31.

119. "Stephen King, The Art of Fiction No. 189," Christopher Lehmann-Haupt and Nathaniel Rich, *The Paris Review*, Issue 178, Fall 2006. https://www.theparisreview.org/interviews/5653/the-art-of-fiction-no-189-stephen-king, September 17, 2021.

120. "Bleedful Things," Brad Ashton-Haiste, *Fangoria*, August 1991, 28-31.

121. "Stephen King, The Art of Fiction No. 189," Christopher Lehmann-Haupt and Nathaniel Rich, *The Paris Review*, Issue 178, Fall 2006. https://www.theparisreview.org/interviews/5653/the-art-of-fiction-no-189-stephen-king, September 17, 2021.

122. "Digging Up Stories with Stephen King," Wallace Stroby, *Writers On Writing*, September 16, 1991. http://wallacestroby.com/ writersonwriting_king.html, September 19, 2021.

123. "The Writer Defines Himself: An Interview with Stephen King," Tony Magistrale, *Stephen King: the Second Decade, Danse Macabre to The Dark Half*, (Twayne Publishers, 1992), 3.

124. "Stephen King Shines On," Linda Marotta, *Fangoria* #150, March 1996.

125. "Digging Up Stories with Stephen King," Wallace Stroby, *Writers On Writing*, September 16, 1991. http://wallacestroby.com/ writersonwriting_king.html, September 19, 2021.

126. *Nightmares & Dreamscapes* (Viking, 1993), xviii.

127. *Nightmares & Dreamscapes* (Viking, 1993), xxii.

128. *On Writing* (Scribner, 2000), 169.

129. "Stephen King on His Ten Longest Novels," Gilbert Cruz, *Time*, November 6, 2009.https://entertainment.time.com/2009/11/09/ stephen-king-on-his-10-longest-novels/ slide/insomnia-1994/, September 28, 2021.

130. Transcript, alt.books.stephen-king, April 24, 1996. https:// groups.google.com/g/alt.books.stephen-king/c/ Dtq9N8LAL-A/m/bty91c-JRzIJ, October 7, 2021.

131. "Digging Up Stories with Stephen King," Wallace Stroby, *Writers On Writing*, September 16, 1991. http://wallacestroby.com/ writersonwriting_king.html, September 19, 2021.

132. *On Writing* (Scribner, 2000), 169.

133. "Stephen King and his compulsion to write," Anthony Mason, *CBS Sunday Morning*, June 30, 2013. https://www.cbsnews.com/ news/stephen-king-and-his-compulsion-to-write/, September 28, 2021.

134. "Stephen King Shines On," Linda Marotta, *Fangoria* #150, March 1996.

135. Introduction, *The Green Mile* (Plume, 1997), v-viii.

136. Introduction, *The Green Mile* (Plume, 1997), v-viii.

137. Introduction, *The Green Mile: The Two Dead Girls* (Signet, 1996), vii-xiii.

138. Introduction, *The Green Mile: The Two Dead Girls* (Signet, 1996), vii-xiii.

139. Transcript, alt.books.stephen-king, April 24, 1996. https:// groups.google.com/g/alt.books.stephen-king/c/ Dtq9N8LAL-A/m/ bty91c-JRzIJ, October 7, 2021.

140. Introduction, *The Green Mile: The Two Dead Girls* (Signet, 1996), vii-xiii.

141. *On Writing* (Scribner, 2000), 197.

142. "An Evening with Stephen King," *Secret Windows*, (Book-of-the-Month Club, 2000), 387-401.

143. "King of the Season," Judy Quinn, *Publishers Weekly Guide to Fall Books 1996*, Fall 1996, 293.

144. "Stephen King's God Trip," John Marks, *Salon*, October 23, 2008, https://www.salon.com/2008/10/23/ stephen_king/September 11, 2021.

145. "Stephen King on His 10 Longest Novels," Gilbert Cruz, *Time*, November 6, 2009. https://entertainment.time.com/2009/11/09/ stephen-king-on-his-10-longest-novels/ slide/desperation-1996/, September 30, 2021.

146. "The Importance of Being Bachman," *The Bachman Books* (NAL, 1996), 7.

147. "The Importance of Being Bachman," *The Bachman Books* (NAL, 1996), 7.

148. *The Book Reporter*, November 21, 1997. https:// web.archive.org/web/20090121183426/http://teenreads. com:80/authors/au-king-stephen.asp, April 4, 2024.

149. "Secrets, Lies and *Bag of Bones*," Amazon.com, October 1998, http://www.geocities.com/willemfh/king/ mail_king.htm, April 4, 2009.

150. "Love, Death and Stephen King," Amazon.com, 1998, https://77www.oocities.org/heartland/bluffs/7745/king/ interview_king.htm, April 4, 2024.

151. "Stephen King, The Art of Fiction No. 189," Christopher Lehmann-Haupt and Nathaniel Rich, *The Paris Review*, Issue 178, Fall 2006. https://www. theparisreview.org/interviews/5653/the-art-of-fiction-no-189-stephen-king, September 17, 2021.

152. "Weathering Heights," Michael Rowe, *Fangoria* 181 (April 1999), 34-38.

153. "Love, Death and Stephen King," Amazon.com, 1998. https://77www.oocities.org/heartland/bluffs/7745/king/ interview_king.htm, April 4, 2024.

154. "The Salon Interview," Andrew O'Hehir, *Salon*, September 24, 1998, https://www.salon. com/1998/09/24/cov_si_24int/, September 18, 2021.

155. Letter to Readers, Scribner website, April 1998. http://www.litteraturesdelimaginaire.com/_dossiers/sac. html, September 18, 2021.

156. "King homers off Gordon," Joseph P. Kahn, *Boston Globe*, April 28, 1999, E01.

157. "King homers off Gordon," Joseph P. Kahn, *Boston Globe*, April 28, 1999, E01.

158. "King homers off Gordon," Joseph P. Kahn, *Boston Globe*, April 28, 1999, E01.

159. "King homers off Gordon," Joseph P. Kahn, *Boston Globe*, April 28, 1999, E01.

160. "Novel comes as no relief for King, Gordon," Ron Rapoport, *Chicago Sun-Times*, December 26, 2000. https://chicagosuntimes. newsbank.com/doc/news/0EB424B5A15592D6?pdate=2000-12-26, September 19, 2021.

161. "Dear Constant Readers," (Scribner 1999).

162. "Stephen King Scares Up His Past," Marion Long, *Mary Higgins Clark Mystery Magazine*, v26 #6, Summer 2000, 4.

163. Interview with Stanley Wiater, Barnes and Noble, September 1998.

164. *On Writing* (Scribner, 2000), 254.

165. *On Writing* (Scribner, 2000), 256.

166. Interview with Bryant Gumbel, *The Early Show*, March 20, 2001.

167. *On Writing* (Scribner, 2000), 267.

168. "House Master," Kim Murphy, *Los Angeles Times*, January 27, 2002, F-3. https://www.latimes.com/archives/la-xpm-2002-jan-27-ca-murphy27-story.html. September 14, 2021.

169. YouTube, https://www.youtube.com/watch?v=fLB8Rx6FzOE, October 7, 2021.

170. *On Writing* (Scribner, 2000), 265.

171. *On Writing* (Scribner, 2000), 286.

172. "The Stephen King interview, uncut and unpublished," Tim Adams, *The Guardian*, September 14, 2000. https://www. theguardian.com/books/2000/sep/14/stephenking.fiction, September 15, 2021.

173. Author's Note, *Dreamcatcher* (Scribner, 2001), 619-620.

174. Author's Note, *Dreamcatcher* (Scribner, 2001), 619-620.

175. "Stephen King on His 10 Longest Novels," Gilbert Cruz, *Time*, November 6, 2009. https://entertainment.time.com/2009/11/09/ stephen-king-on-his-10-longest-novels/slide/dreamcatcher-2001/, September 15, 2021.

176. "Stephen King: The *Rolling Stone* Interview," Andy Greene, *Rolling Stone*, October 31, 2014. https://www.rollingstone. com/culture/culture-features/stephen-king-the-rolling-stone- interview-191529/, September 15, 2021.

177. *Everything's Eventual* (Scribner, 2001), Table of Contents.

178. Afterword, *From a Buick 8* (Scribner, 2003), 213.

179. Interview with Joyce Lynch Dewes Moore, Mystery (March 1981). Reprinted in *Bare Bones*, Tim Underwood and Chuck Miller, eds. (McGraw-Hill, 1988), 68-76.

180. Afterword, *From a Buick 8* (Scribner, 2003), 213-214.

181. "Retirement, the Stephen King way: writing, not publishing," Marshall Fine, *The (Westchester, N.Y.) News Journal*, October 13, 2002. https://archive.seattletimes. com/archive/?date=20021013&slug=wstephenking13, September 15, 2021.

182. "House Master," Kim Murphy, *Los Angeles Times*, January 27, 2002. https://www.latimes.com/archives/la-xpm-2002-jan-27-ca-murphy27-story.html, September 15, 2021.

183. "10 Questions for Stephen King," Andrea Sachs, *Time*, March 24, 2002. http://content.time.com/time/magazine/article/0,9171,219787,00.html, September 15, 2021.

184. *Faithful* (Scribner, 2004), 246.

185. "New Book by Stephen King to Kick Off Hard Case Crime's Second Year," Official website, February 28, 2005. https://stephenking.com/news/new-book-by-stephen-king-to-kick-off-hard-case-crimes-second-year-54.html, September 16, 2021.

186. "Cover boys," Madeleine Murray, *The Sydney Morning Herald*, December 29, 2005. https://www.smh. com.au/entertainment/books/cover-boys-20051229-gdmp9b.html, September 17, 2021.

187. "A Grand Master, Indeed, Ridley Pearson," *The 3rd Degree* (Mystery Writers of America newsletter), November 2006, 5.

188. "King of Sox fans has novel concept," Dan Shaughnessy, *The Boston Globe*, February 20, 1999.

189. "Cemetery Dance Publications Announces *Blockade Billy* by Stephen King," Press Release. https://www.prnewswire.com/news-releases/cemetery-dance-publications-announces-blockade-billy-by-stephen-king-89501162.html, September 12, 2021.

190. "King of Sox fans has novel concept," Dan Shaughnessy, *The Boston Globe*, February 20, 1999.

191. *Cell* (Scribner, 2006), 172.

192. "Stephen King, The Art of Fiction No. 189," Christopher Lehmann-Haupt and Nathaniel Rich, *The Paris Review*, Issue 178, Fall 2006. https://www.theparisreview.org/interviews/5653/the-art-of-fiction-no-189-stephen-king, September 17, 2021.

193. "Stephen King Tries to Ring Up Book Sales," Jeffrey A. Trachtenberg, *The Wall Street Journal*, January 17, 2016. https://www.wsj.com/articles/SB113745182031647918, September 17, 2021.

194. "The Once and Future Stephen King," Jill Owens, powells.com, November 2006. https://www.powells.com/post/interviews/the-once-and-future-stephen-king, September 15, 2021.

195. "How Lisey Found Her Story," Ben P. Indick, *Publishers Weekly*, August 28, 2006. https://www.publishersweekly.com/pw/by-topic/authors/interviews/article/16357-how-lisey-found-her-story.html, September 15, 2021.

196. Interview with Mark Lawson, BBC Four, December 11, 2006.

197. Afterword, *Lisey's Story* (Scribner, 2006), 511-512.

198. The Once and Future Stephen King," Jill Owens, powells.com, November 2006. https://www.powells.com/post/interviews/the-once-and-future-stephen-king, September 15, 2021.

199. Afterword, *Different Seasons* (Viking, 1982), 323.

200. Afterword, *Different Seasons* (Viking, 1982), 323.

201. Introduction, *Blaze*, (Scribner, 2007), 3-5.

202. Introduction, *Blaze*, (Scribner, 2007), 3-5.

203. "Quint's chat with Stephen King," Eric Vespe (a.k.a. Quint), *Ain't it Cool News*, February 27, 2007. http://legacy.aintitcool.com/node/31707, September 18, 2021.

204. Introduction to *Just After Sunset* (Scribner, 2008), 3.

205. "At 60, horror writer Stephen King accepts that he's no longer middle-aged," AP, January 20, 2008. https://www.winnipegfreepress.com/historic/2008/01/19/at-60-horror-writer-stephen-king-accepts-that-hes-no-longer-middle-aged, September 15, 2021.

206. "King's New Realm," Gilbert Cruz, *Time*, January 17, 2008. http://content.time.com/time/subscriber/article/0,33009,1704697,00.html, September 15, 2021.

207. "*Duma Key* finds Stephen King stepping into his own life," Bob Minzesheimer, *USA Today*, January 24, 2008. https://horrorthon.blogspot.com/2008/01/duma-key-finds-stephen-king-stepping.html, September 15, 2021.

208. "At 60, horror writer Stephen King accepts that he's no longer middle-aged," AP, January 20, 2008. https://dailyillini.com/features/2008/01/21/at-60-horror-writer-stephen-king-accepts-that-hes-no-longer-middle-aged/, September 15, 2021.

209. "*Duma Key* finds Stephen King stepping into his own life," Bob Minzesheimer, *USA Today*, January 24, 2008. https://horrorthon.blogspot.com/2008/01/duma-key-finds-stephen-king-stepping.html, September 15, 2021.

210. "Stephen King on His 10 Longest Novels," Gilbert Cruz, *Time*, November 6, 2009. https://entertainment.time.com/2009/11/09/stephen-king-on-his-10-longest-novels/slide/duma-key-2008/, September 15, 2021.

211. "Stephen King and Family Speak at the Library," April 04, 2008. https://www.loc.gov/item/webcast-4302/, September 16, 2021.

212. *The Art of Darkness*, Douglas E. Winter (NAL, 1984), 157.

213. "*The Stand* Is a Cornucopia of Stephen King Easter Eggs (If You Know Where to Look)," Josh Weiss, *Forbes*, February 12, 2021. https://www.forbes.com/sites/joshweiss/2021/02/12/the-stand-is-a-cornucopia-of-stephen-king-easter-eggs-if-you-know-where-to-look/?sh=1f3c7a336a66, September 22, 2021.

214. Afterword, *Full Dark, No Stars* (Scribner, 2010), 365.

215. "Stephen King unearths origin of *The Shining* sequel *Doctor Sleep*," Anthony Brenzican, *Entertainment Weekly*, February 1, 2013, https://ew.com/article/2013/02/01/stephen-king-the-shining-doctor-sleep-preview/ September 11, 2021.

216. Message from Steve – *Doctor Sleep*, March 2, 2012, https://web.archive.org/web/20120325075611/http://www.stephenking.com/news.html, April 4, 2024.

217. "Stephen King on Growing Up, Believing in God and Getting Scared," by Terry Gross, *Fresh Air*, May 28, 2013. https://www.npr.org/2013/05/28/184827647/stephen-king-on-growing-up-believing-in-god-and-getting-scared, September 11, 2021.

218. "Stephen King novel *Joyland* officially announced," Stephan Lee, *Entertainment Weekly*, May 30, 2012, https://ew.com/article/2012/09/20/stephen-king-joyland/, September 11, 2021.

219. "Stephen King talks new novel *Later*, kid protagonists and storytelling during COVID-19." Brian Truitt, *USA Today*, March 1, 2021. https://www.usatoday.com/story/entertainment/books/2021/03/01/stephen-king-talks-new-novel-later-covid-storytelling/6815490002/, September 11, 2021.

220. "Stephen King talks about crime, creativity and new novel," by Hillel Italie, AP News, February 25, 2021. https://apnews.com/article/stephen-king-later-new-crime-book-b4ec29efb4c3183f1e565 575a54ae777 September 11, 2021.

221. "Interview with Stephen King," Goodreads, November 5, 2014. https://www.goodreads.com/interviews/show/989.Stephen_King, September 28, 2021.

222. "Stephen King on new book, playing in a band," *Morning Joe*, MSNBC, November 12, 2014. https://www.msnbc.com/morning-joe/watch/stephen-king-on-new-book--playing-in-a-band-356885059539, September 28, 2021.

223. "Master of horror Stephen King talks baseball, his latest book *Revival* and how he's not done yet," John Holyoke, *Bangor Daily News*, November 7, 2014. https://www.pressherald.com/2014/11/14/king-talks-baseball-revival-writing-retirement/, September 28, 2021.

224. "How Gwendy Escaped Oblivion," Foreword to *Gwendy's Magic Feather* by Richard Chizmar (Cemetery Dance 2019), 7.

225. "Pennywise's creator on scaring the hell out of 2017," Anthony Brenzican, *Entertainment Weekly*, December 22, 2017.

226. "Writing Rapture," Jessica Strawser, *Writers Digest*, May/June 2009, 48.

227. "Things get doubly freaky when Stephen King and son Joe Hill team up 'In the Tall Grass.'" Brian Truitt *USA Today*, October 3, 2019. https://www.usatoday.com/story/entertainment/movies/2019/10/03/stephen-king-joe-hill-give-netflix-scare-in-tall-grass/3835164002/, October 3, 2021.

228. "How Stephen King and son Owen joined forces in the nightmare business for *Sleeping Beauties*," Anthony Brenzican, *Entertainment Weekly*, September 25, 2017. https://ew.com/books/2017/09/25/stephen-king-owen-king-sleeping-beauties/, October 3, 2021.

229. "Stephen King on killer clowns, *Stranger Things*, and his secrets for scaring you silly," Nick Schager, AP, September 6, 2017. https://www.yahoo.com/entertainment/stephen-king-killer-clowns-stranger-things-secrets-scaring-silly-153305101.html, October 3, 2021.

230. "Writing Rapture," Jessica Strawser, *Writers Digest*, May/June 2009, 48.

231. "Stephen King holds court in Sarasota," Jimmy Geurts, *Sarasota Herald Tribune*, March 15, 2017. https://www.heraldtribune.com/news/20170315/exclusive-stephen-king-talks-new-book-movies-in-sarasota, October 2, 2021.

232. "Stephen King, The Art of Fiction No. 189," Christopher Lehmann-Haupt and Nathaniel Rich, *The Paris Review*, Issue 178, Fall 2006. https://www.theparisreview.org/interviews/5653/the-art-of-fiction-no-189-stephen-king, September 17, 2021.

233. "Stephen King on Why *Lisey's Story* Was One He Had to Adapt Himself," Erik Piepenburg, *The New York Times*, June 3, 2021. https://www.nytimes.com/2021/06/03/arts/television/liseys-story-stephen-king-apple.html, October 2, 2021.

234. "Life Is Imitating Stephen King's Art, and That Scares Him," Anthony Brenzican, *The New York Times*, September 3, 2019. https://www.nytimes.com/2019/09/03/books/stephen-king-interview-the-institute.html, October 2, 2021.

235. Author Note, *If It Bleeds*, (Scribner, 2020), 433.

236. Author Note, *If It Bleeds*, (Scribner, 2020), 434.

237. "Even Stephen King Can't Escape a Quarantine That Feels Like Living in a Stephen King Book," Anthony Brenzican, *Vanity Fair*, April 28, 2020. https://www.vanityfair.com/culture/2020/04/stephen-king-trump-quarantine-the-stand-if-it-bleeds, October 2, 2021.

238. Stephen King Takes Us Inside the Process of Writing *Billy Summers,* Adrienne Westenfeld, *Esquire*, Aug 3, 2021. https://www.esquire.com/entertainment/books/a37182078/stephen-king-billy-summers-interview/, October 2, 2021.

239. Stephen King Takes Us Inside the Process of Writing *Billy Summers,* Adrienne Westenfeld, *Esquire*, Aug 3, 2021. https://www.esquire.com/entertainment/books/a37182078/stephen-king-billy-summers-interview/, October 2, 2021.

240. "Stephen King Dreamed Up a Hitman. Then King Let Him Take on a Life of His Own," Brenna Ehrlich, *Rolling Stone*, August 3, 2021. https://www.rollingstone.com/culture/culture-features/stephen-king-billy-summers-interview-1203646/, October 2, 2021.

241. "Read an exclusive excerpt from Stephen King's forthcoming novel *Fairy Tale*," Clark Collis, *Entertainment Weekly*, January 24, 2022, https://ew.com/books/stephen-king-fairy-tale-new-novel-excerpt/, March 12, 2022.

242. "Stephen King Knows Anti-Vaxxers Are Going to Hate His Latest Book: 'Knock Yourself Out'," Brenna Ehrlich, Rolling Stone, September 5, 2023. https://www.msn.com/en-us/tv/news/stephen-king-knows-anti-vaxxers-are-going-to-hate-his-latest-book-knock-yourself-out/ar-AA1ghh2V, March 17, 2024.

243. "*It* Trailer Scares Up Worldwide Traffic Record in First 24 Hours with Near 200M," Anthony D'Alessandro, *Deadline*, March 31, 2017. https://deadline.com/2017/03/it-stephen-king-trailer-traffic-record-warner-bros-new-line-1202056928/, October 4, 2021.

244. Interview with Hans-Åke Lilja, *Lilja's Library*, January 18, 2007, http://www.liljas-library.com/showinterview.php?id=36, October 1, 2021.

245. "Stephen King talks about crime, creativity and new novel," Hillel Italie, AP News, February 25, 2021. https://apnews.com/article/stephen-king-later-new-crime-book-b4ec29efb4c3183f1e565575a54ae777, September 11, 2021.

246. "Stephen King's New Monster," Alexandra Alter, *The Wall Street Journal*, October 28, 2011. https://www.wsj.com/articles/SB10001424052970204644504576651540980143566, October 7, 2021.

247. "Stephen King: 'I have outlived most of my critics. It gives me great pleasure,'" Xan Brooks, *Guardian*, September 7, 2019. https://www.theguardian.com/books/2019/sep/07/stephen-king-interview-the-institute, September 29, 2021.

248. "Stephen King talks about crime, creativity and new novel," Hillel Italie, AP News, February 25, 2021. https://apnews.com/article/stephen-king-later-new-crime-book-b4ec29efb4c3183f1e565575a54ae777, September 11, 2021.

IMAGE CREDITS

Page 9 Andre Jenny / Alamy Stock Photo

Page 10 Courtesy of Stephen King

Page 13 Courtesy of Stephen King

Page 14 Courtesy of Stephen King

Page 15 Courtesy of Stephen King

Page 16 Courtesy of Stephen King

Page 19 Courtesy of Stephen King

Page 21 Courtesy of Bob Jackson

Page 23 Courtesy of Bob Jackson

Page 25 Courtesy of Doubleday Publishing Group

Page 26 Peter Jones / Contributor/getty

page 26 (right) Courtesy of Stephen King

Page 28 Courtesy of Stephen King

Page 30 Courtesy of Doubleday Publishing Group

Page 33 Courtesy of Bob Jackson

Page 34 Peter Jones / Contributor/getty

Page 35 Sunset Boulevard / Contributor/getty

Page 37 Courtesy of Penguin Random House

Page 40 (top) Bridgeman Images; (bottom) Courtesy of Doubleday/ Publishing Group

Page 43 Courtesy of Stephen King

Page 44 Courtesy of Stephen King

Page 45 Courtesy of Stephen King

Page 46 United Archives GmbH / Alamy Stock Photo

Page 48 Moviestore Collection Ltd / Alamy Stock Photo

Page 49 Pictorial Press Ltd / Alamy Stock Photo

Page 53 Allstar Picture Library Ltd / Alamy Stock Photo

Page 54 Buddy Mays / Alamy Stock Photo

Page 55 Courtesy of Stephen King

Page 56 Maximum Film / Alamy Stock Photo (left)

Page 56 Courtesy of Jim Leonard (right)

Page 66 (top) RGR Collection / Alamy Stock Photo (bottom) Courtesy of Jim Leonard

Page 69 Courtesy of Penguin Random House

Page 70 ©Paramount/courtesy Everett Collection

Page 73 Courtesy of Doubleday Publishing Group

ABOUT THE AUTHOR

Bev Vincent is a contributing editor with *Cemetery Dance* magazine, where he has been writing the column "Stephen King: News from the Dead Zone" since 2001. He is a two-time Bram Stoker award nominee and has also been nominated for the Edgar, ITW Thriller, and Ignotus Awards. In addition to this book, he is the author of *The Road to the Dark Tower* and *The Dark Tower Companion*, and co-editor of *Flight or Fright* with Stephen King. He has also published over one hundred short stories, dozens of essays, and hundreds of book reviews. His screenplay for the "dollar baby" film *Stephen King's Gotham Café*, cowritten with two other writers, was named Best Adaptation at the International Horror and Sci-Fi Film Festival in 2004. His website is www.bevvinvent.com.

ACKNOWLEDGMENTS

This book was produced and brought to market with the great assistance and encouragement from these people at Quarto: Delia Greve, Haley Stocking, Cara Donaldson, Rage Kindelsperger, and Steve Roth, along with many others whose names I never learned. It takes a lot of people to put together a book like this. Special thanks to Sarah Fabiny for helping me adapt the book for young readers.

I would like to thank Marsha DeFilippo, Stephen King's personal assistant, now retired, who has been a wonderful resource for me over the years. I tried not to bug her too much, but she always had the answers to my questions when I posed them. Julie Eugley provided recent material from Stephen King's archives.

My literary agent, Michael Psaltis, is the kind of person every writer wants to have on his side. It's an endless source of encouragement to know someone else out there has my future as a writer on his radar. My wife, Mary Anne, is my number one fan, and I'm hers. Always. I would like to dedicate this book to a new generation of young readers, some of whom may discover the joy of reading through Stephen King's books and stories, including most especially my grandchildren, Helen Margaret Ball and Henry Amos Ball.

I picked up a copy of *'Salem's Lot* in a secondhand bookstore in Halifax, Nova Scotia, in 1979. I can't recall any of the other books I purchased that day, but that little black paperback with the drop of red blood was the beginning of my avid interest in the works of Stephen King. At least once every year since then, I've had the pleasure of reading a new novel from him. I've often said if he decided to write romance novels, I would still read his books because for me it's all about the characters. Thank you for decades of entertainment, and I hope there will be many more to come.

© 2022, 2024 by Quarto Publishing Group USA Inc.
Text © 2022, 2024 by Bev Vincent

First published in 2024 by becker&mayer!kids, an imprint of The Quarto Group,
142 West 36th Street, 4th Floor, New York, NY 10018, USA
(212) 779-4972 www.Quarto.com

Contains content previously published as *Stephen King* in 2022 by Epic Ink, an imprint of
The Quarto Group,142 West 36th Street, 4th Floor, New York, NY 10018, USA.

becker&mayer!kids titles are also available at discount for retail, wholesale, promotional, and bulk purchase. For details,
contact the Special Sales Manager by email at specialsales@quarto.com or by mail at The Quarto Group, Attn: Special
Sales Manager, 100 Cummings Center Suite 265D, Beverly, MA 01915 USA.

10 9 8 7 6 5 4 3 2 1

ISBN: 978-0-7603-8772-6

Digital edition published in 2024
eISBN: 978-0-7603-8773-3

Library of Congress Cataloging-in-Publication Data

Names: Vincent, Bev, author.
Title: Stephen King : his life, work, and influences / Bev Vincent.
Description: Young readers' edition. | New York : becker&mayer!kids, 2024.
  | Includes bibliographical references. | Audience: Ages 12. | Audience:
  Grades 7-9. | Summary: "Stephen King: His Life, Work, and Influences
  offers young Stephen King fans a thrilling journey through the writer's
  personal story and its impact on his work"-- Provided by publisher.
Identifiers: LCCN 2024006015 (print) | LCCN 2024006016 (ebook) | ISBN
  9780760387726 (paperback) | ISBN 9780760387733 (ebook)
Subjects: LCSH: King, Stephen, 1947---Juvenile literature. | Authors,
  American--Biography--Juvenile literature. | Horror tales,
  American--History and criticism--Juvenile literature.
Classification: LCC PS3561.I483 Z897 2024 (print) | LCC PS3561.I483
  (ebook) | DDC 813/.54--dc23/eng/20240213
LC record available at https://lccn.loc.gov/2024006015
LC ebook record available at https://lccn.loc.gov/2024006016

Group Publisher: Rage Kindelsperger
Editorial Director: Lori Burke
Creative Director: Laura Drew
Managing Editor: Cara Donaldson
Editor: Sarah Fabiny
Cover and Interior Design: Kim Winscher

Printed in China

Lexile®: 1110L

MIX
Paper | Supporting
responsible forestry
FSC® C016973